DATE DUE

DEMCO 38-296

ISBN: No. 1-901230-03-1

Copyright © ISLAMIC WORLD REPORT 1997

PHOTOGRAPH: Frank Spooner Pictures

ISLAMIC WORLD REPORT

PO BOX 9811 LONDON W11 3GD

ALGERIA

Revolution Revisited

EDITORIAL ADVISORY BOARD

CONTENTS

INTRODUCTION

ALGERIA:

REVOLUTION REVISITED

Algeria is a nation beset with endemic – one might almost say systemic – violence: extra-judicial killings and routinized torture by a state claiming to be legitimate, monstrous acts of terrorism by groups calling themselves 'Islamic'. In the past four years, approximately 100,000 people have been killed, that is, on average, 500 people every week, with countless more maimed, injured, and traumatized. How is one to explain this explosion of violence, on the one hand, and this exploitation and distortion of Islam, on the other? The relationship between Islam and the current crisis in Algeria, as elsewhere in the Muslim world, is all too often studied from a viewpoint determined exclusively by political analysis, so that what enters into this frame of reference is simply Islam such as it has been politicized, exploited, or disfigured. Some light will of course be shed on the immediate causes of the current crisis by a careful political analysis of the events preceding it – the increasing pressure for democracy in the late 1980s, the growth of the 'Islamist' movement, its success in the local elections of 1990, the annulment of the general elections of 1991 by the army, and the subsequent repression of the Islamist groups – but the more profound causes of the crisis will not be revealed by such an analysis, neither will the underlying religious dynamics within the 'Islamist' movement be rendered any clearer. What is needed is an approach which locates these immediate political causes within a framework defined both by history and by culture, taking this word in its widest meaning.

1

The present volume takes a step towards the articulation of such an approach by bringing together essays which deal with different aspects of the Algerian crisis: historical, social, cultural, political, religious, and spiritual. In so doing, it brings to light certain essential features of the forms that political Islam has assumed in Algeria, and at the same time provides a critique of these forms 'from within', that is, from a perspective proper to traditional Islam.

The crisis through which the country is now passing cannot be understood without taking full account of the intense violence – physical, psychological, cultural, and spiritual – to which the Algerians were subject for over one hundred years under the French. The forces unleashed by western colonialism disrupted and dislocated Muslim peoples throughout the world; but it can confidently be asserted that none have been more deeply traumatized by the colonial experience than the Algerian Muslims. For it was in Algeria above all that the French tried to implement their *mission civilisatrice* ('civilising mission'). Nowhere else was the policy of assimilation carried through with such relentless rigour, in no other conquered territory did France hang on to power so tenaciously – a million people died in the 1954-62 War of Liberation. The ethos underlying the French colonial enterprise in Algeria was put bluntly by Dr Bopichon, author of two books on Algeria in the 1840s:

> Little does it matter that France in her political conduct goes beyond the limits of common morality at times; the essential thing is that she establish a lasting colony, and that as a consequence she will bring European civilization to these barbarous countries; when a project which is to the advantage of all humanity is to be carried out, the shortest path is the best. Now, it is certain that the shortest path is terror ...[1]

Whatever the protestations of the French that their intention was not to destroy Algerian society but to raise it up to the level of France, in concrete terms the colonial project of assimilating Algeria to France pre-supposed the elimination of the essential elements of Algeria's tradition, its culture, and its personality: all of which was determined by the religion of Islam. Hence, quite naturally, it was Islam that was regarded by the French as the obstacle in the way of full assimilation. The first essay here, by Rashid Messaoudi, charts the story of the civilizational hegemony exercised by France over Algeria, and how French influence has persisted even after the official decolonization of Algeria. Much of what he discloses will no doubt open the eyes of many in the western world who assumed that decolonization meant an end to the domination of Algeria by France. Overt power was, as he demonstrates, replaced by covert influence, exercised through a francophile elite, the extent of whose corruption has been known only to very few. The second essay, by Omar Benaissa, also focuses on the colonial period, but from a very different perspective. He demonstrates the important role played by the Sufis first in fighting the French militarily and then in resisting them culturally and spiritually. He shows in the process the falsity of the notion – all too current in modern Muslim circles – that the Sufis were lackeys of imperialism, 'marabouts' who kept the masses steeped in ignorance and superstition, feeding them the religious opium that dulled their political senses, all to the benefit of the colonialists. We shall return, in the concluding essay of the volume, to the role of Sufism in relation both to colonialism and formal Islam, a role which, however limited be the attention given to it hitherto, is of fundamental importance if one wishes to understand the contemporary crisis of Islam in Algeria and elsewhere in the Muslim world.

The next two essays focus more directly on the political unfolding of the contemporary crisis. Mohamed Gharib offers a very important overview of the different political strands and tendencies that make up the Islamist movement, arguing that, although the extremists seize the headlines with their outrages, the bulk of the Islamists are in fact dedicated to peaceful political processes, constituting a silent majority that is being outflanked by the extremist wing of the movement, on the one hand, and decimated by the security forces, on the other. Looking at the conflict between Islamism and the state from the other side, as it were, George Joffé's essay focuses on the echelon of the Algerian state that is primarily responsible for the present onslaught against the Islamists: the military establishment. He shows how the 'eradicators' within the military have prevailed over the rival faction of 'conciliators', and he traces the origins of the process by which the military have come to play such a decisive role in the independent Algerian state.

In her essay on Sufism in contemporary Algeria, Sossie Andezian argues that the current affirmation of political Islam should not be allowed to eclipse the resurfacing of the Sufi brotherhoods, especially in rural areas. Through the influence of orientalism, Sufism has long been considered as possessing only a historical interest, its contemporary manifestations being treated as forms of atavism, to be studied anthropologically. This essay, on the contrary, shows the extent to which the spiritual content of Sufism is woven into the social fabric of local communities, a fabric made all the more durable by the persistence of Sufism throughout the post-independence period, even though this influence has become more palpable only in the 1990s. The following essay, by Brahim Nali, discusses the Berber issue. Taking a broad historical perspective, he counsels his fellow Berbers to concentrate on the cultural aspects of Berber identity and not to fall into political 'Berberism'; to re-integrate this identity within the universal framework of Islam, and avoid an ethnically-based exclusivism that would but be the mirror-image of the 'Arabization' programme launched by the regime in the 1970s.

The essay by Michèle Messaoudi deals with the cultural heritage of Algeria. She stresses that culture is not to be reduced to that which simply fills the leisure time of a minority; rather, it is that which gives meaningful content to the essential activities of a people. One might add that, traditionally, it is religion that will define what is 'essential' within any culture; and part of the Algerian tragedy is the fact that, having been alienated from the spiritual roots of their tradition, generations of Algerians have sought 'culture' in western models; and, what is more pernicious because less easily discerned, culture itself, as a separate, autonomous, and largely secular domain has been proposed as the source of freedom and fulfilment, displacing that fountain of creative inspiration that religion comprises in its essence.

The editor concludes the volume with an essay on the implicit secularization of Islam wrought by Muslim modernists in Algeria, a process that informs the ideological background of the rise of Muslim extremism. It is argued that, in the name of purifying Islam of Sufi 'maraboutism', the Muslim reformists unwittingly contributed to the desacralization of the religion, which in turn facilitated the politicization of Islam and its reduction to an ideology; and, in promoting the idea of national identity in the pursuit of liberation from French rule, the unintended but nonetheless baneful consequence was the marginalization of religious consciousness, especially in respect of the politically active groups in society. The current violence perpetrated by terrorists in the name of Islam cannot be fully comprehended without taking account of the way in which religion was, on the one hand, reduced to an ideology, and, on the other, displaced by nationalism.～

The Editor

NOTES

1. Quoted in W.B. Quandt, *Revolution and Political Leadership: Algeria, 1954-68*, M.I.T. Press, Cambridge, Mass. p.4.

CHAPTER I

ALGERIAN-FRENCH RELATIONS:
1830-1991
A CLASH OF CIVILIZATIONS

Rashid Messaoudi

From the point of view of those Algerian Muslims who are proud of their tradition and their culture, the history of Algerian-French relations is one of civilizational hegemony, cultural enslavement and depersonalization from the beginning of colonization to the present day. This basic view was at the root of the massive electoral success given to the newly set up Islamic Salvation Front (FIS) in the elections of 1990 and 1991, by the people of Algeria after having been subjected for over thirty years to westernization through French culture and language, and through various shades of Marxist ideology. The imminent election of an Islamist government was, however, thwarted by a military coup, supported and upheld by the French government. This anti-Islamic action by the French conforms to a distinct historical pattern that any objective investigation of French-Algerian relations would clearly reveal. This is a pattern dominated by the various French endeavours to eliminate the central components of the Islamic identity of the Algerian people through economic, cultural, and political domination.

Algeria was traditionally part of the greater Maghreb, formerly known as *Ifriqīyya*. West Africa was Islamized by the Maghrebi *Murābiṭūn*, the *Saʿdīyya* and the *Tijānīyya* Sufi orders; there were thus close religious ties between the two regions. France, through various agreements, not only cut this relation between West Africa and the Maghreb, but also divided the Maghreb itself into various countries with a view to weakening Islam systematically, seen from the outset as an antagonistic civilizational factor. In a letter addressed to the French Foreign Minister Guizot, the French representative on the 1845 Borders Committee stated:

> We can only rejoice in the outcome of these negotiations: I was able to drag the Maghrebi delegation to the fort of Lalla Maghniya to endorse, under the barrels of French cannon, the partition of an integral Muslim soil, indeed the partition of one integral Muslim people for the first time in history.[1]

As we cover this topic, our argument is that, apart from the 'compensation complex'[2], the ambition to play the role of world – or at least imperial – *gendarme*, and the usually invoked need for new resources and market outlets, relations between France and Algeria are based first and foremost on one important criterion, which is civilizational: France's arrogation of the right and duty of carrying out a *mission civilisatrice* to the 'inferior races.'[3] This mission was executed with great intensity in the Islamic societies of the Arab world in general and of the Maghreb in particular. But Islam was and remains *the* obstacle to France's civilizational designs. Hicham Djait explains:

> France can scarcely represent the West, but of all the Western countries, it is doubtless the one that had the most contact with Islam in the Mediterranean basin – and hence the one that opposed Islam most passionately.[4]

The Islamic factor has constantly been in the background of France's policy towards Algeria. And it is on this basis that France has attempted to eradicate the Islamic character of Algerian society ever since it colonized it, and tried to detach Algeria from the Arab-Muslim world through propaganda and the education of a francophile elite, claimed to be representative of the Algerian people[5] and which is popularly dubbed *Hizb Fransa* (France's party). The fact that there has been constant resistance to this policy in the name of Islam has led to a sustained French enmity to Algeria which has continued into the present. This antagonism, although 'invisible' in the first two decades or so of independent Algeria, will become quite obvious from 1988 onwards, when Paris resorted to open conflict with the now strong Islamic renaissance movement. But first let us investigate how and in what circumstances this adversarial relationship began between Algeria and France.

FROM COLONIALISM TO INDEPENDENCE: 1830-1962

Algeria was an exporter of wheat to France prior to the French invasion in 1830. The 1789 French revolution was in fact sustained thanks to Algerian wheat[6] for which the French refused to pay, even years after the revolution. The expulsion of the French consul from Algiers as retaliation for the non-payment of debt was used by the French as an excuse for invading Algeria on 5th July 1830. Roger Garaudy sums up what happened next:

> Thus there was imposed on a Muslim country, whose religion forbids alcohol, the monoculture of the vine. Thus was the practice of the subsistence economy terminated. Algeria, from an exporter of wheat, became an importer. Henceforth its dependence [on France] was doubly secured at the economic level: to export its wine, which it did not need, and to import the wheat, which it needed.[7]

Algeria was invaded in June 1830. French historians allege that this invasion was motivated by a French compensation complex,[8] as well as 'an improvized expedient and an internal policy move made by a government in difficulty, in search of a prestige-boosting operation.'[9] Ahmed Mahsas, a sociologist and former nationalist and senior FLN leader, rejects this argument and affirms that the invasion 'was inseparable from the European expansionist movement ... an operation long premeditated against the Arab-Islamic world.'[10]

Thus began an occupation that confirms Mr. Mahsas's argument since the French set out systematically to undermine the very fabric of Algerian society. Colonization began with the occupation of the port cities. Then attempts were made to take over the country gradually. Resistance to the invasion was initially organized around the Emir Abdelkader ben Mahieddin who succeeded in rallying the tribes of western Algeria. He is reported to have said, when he was appointed Emir, that he accepted the position, but that he was ready to stand behind anyone else ready to take up the banner of Islam's cause. Abdelkader was a Ṣufi *ʿālim* of the *Qādirīyya* order, a poet and a man of letters, and was to become Algeria's most famous *mujāhid* and statesman.[11]

The Emir Abdelkader, as Roger Garaudy says, 'knew, by virtue of the highest Islamic tradition, how to link faith and politics. The mystical moment was, for him, that of a 're-centring' on God. His action, as a war leader and statesman, was the expression of his faith and his spirituality for fashioning the world according to God's "guidance".'[12]

Abdelkader resisted for 15 years during which time he signed agreements with the French military leaders who constantly cheated him whose own word was always a commitment.[13] The French practised a virulent 'scorched earth' policy and eventually defeated him in 1847. He was again promised to be allowed to emigrate to Syria, but was, instead, jailed in France until 1852 after which he left for Damascus, via a visit to Turkey's Sultan Abdulhamid. He died in 1883 in Damascus where he was buried.

But resistance did not stop throughout the country and was to continue, albeit sporadically, until 1954. In the meantime, the French responded with unprecedented inhumanity against the Algerians – massacring them, dispossessing them and depersonalizing them.

In his book *Pour un dialogue des civilisations*, Roger Garaudy gives ample details of the extent of the ferocity the French showed in Algeria.[14] The Government Inquiry Commision report of 1883 gives a summary of what was taking place:

> We gathered at the estate the possessions of the religious endowment organizations; we sequestered those of a class of inhabitants whom we had promised to respect ... We took away properties without any compensation and, what is more, we went as far as forcing the people who had been expropriated to pay for the demolition of their houses and even of a mosque.
>
> We desecrated the temples, graves, the interior of houses, which

are a sacred retreat among the Muslims.

We massacred people carrying [French official] passes, on a suspicion we slit the throat of entire populations who were later on proven to be innocent; we tried men famous for their holiness in the country, venerated men, because they had enough courage to come and meet our rage in order to intercede on behalf of their unfortunate fellow countrymen; there were men to sentence them and civilized men to have them executed.[15]

Whereas in South America, the Europeans would scalp the Indians to get a financial reward, the French in Algeria would 'harvest' the natives' ears as part of their *'mission civilisatrice'*. In his book *La chasse à l'homme*, Count d'Hérisson describes in this respect the actions of a unit to which he belonged: 'Admittedly, we would bring back a barrel full of ears harvested, pair by pair, on prisoners, friends or foes ... unbelievable cruelties', specifying that 'The natives' ears were for long worth 10 francs a pair, and their women remained a perfect prey.' In just one year three French colonels, Cavaignac, Pélissier and Saint-Arnaud, annihilated three whole tribes, including their men, women, children and cattle, by smoking and burning them to death in the mountain caves where they took refuge. And when someone once went to a general telling him, 'Sir, here is another tribe asking for mercy', the general answered: 'No, there is there, on our right, that brave colonel who has had nothing yet. Let's leave this tribe for him to crush; that will be a score for him; we shall grant mercy afterwards.'[16] After devoting eleven pages of quotations from primary sources relating such horrific scenes, Garaudy makes the following altogether pertinent comment:

I do not believe that I must apologise for the length of these quotations, because they are mentioned in no textbook, and the consequences of these official silences are well-known regarding the conditioning of minds over the recent episodes of the wars of Indochina and Algeria.[17]

Alongside these material ravages the action which caused the greatest psychological damage was the persistent French attempt to depersonalize the Algerian character. Whereas at the time of invasion, education – in its Islamic form – was just as widespread under the Turkish Regency as in France, by 1848 half the schools had disappeared, according to various eye-witness accounts reported by C. Bontemps.[18] Education was deprived of vital resources and the teachers were pushed into poverty, exiled, or harrassed by Catholic priests. Meanwhile, Arabic-French colleges were created in order to cause the closure of Quranic schools which were places of cultural resistance, Mahsas points out.[19]

The French were, therefore, determined to undermine the basic features of Algerian society, that is, mainly the religion of Islam and the Arabic language. French colonial policy 'attacked in a particular way, the Arab-Islamic culture in which it sees the principal force of resistance to its depersonalization enterprise', while at the same time French education was hardly made available because it was also seen as a weapon of awareness and thus a danger to colonization.[20] When, reluctantly, Muslims did send their children to French-run schools, it was the beginning of a long process that was to alienate an entire elite from its Islamic roots. Monique Gadant confirms this:

> French schooling policy was, despite the goodwill of many school masters, a permanent rape of minds; so was its religious policy through the establishment of a local Church as well as of an Islam controlled by France. Indeed, in Algeria there had been no separation between 'Church' and State. France appointed the imams and exercised severe control over the mosques. [The emergence of] maraboutism was the effect of an introversion as well as of the state of cultural and economic backwardness in which colonialism had pushed the rural populations.[21]

As a consequence of this policy, an ideology of hate 'developed in the cities of Algeria, as in all the Maghreb, expressing the global opposition to cultural integration, the rejection of the French, of their laws and of their customs. Those who were called "Old Turbans" chose to live on with the preservation at all costs of their traditions or through *hijra* [emigration] to the *Dār al-Islām*.'[22]

Meanwhile, Islam was stripped of its cultural infrastructure. Religious endowments were confiscated and mosques and schools destroyed. As a result, religion underwent a great decline and was only maintained thanks to the individual and collective faith practised through the *zāwiyas*.[23] Ahmed Mahsas points out that Catholic propaganda to convert the Muslims went hand in hand with the French government's action to reduce Islam to its simplest expression.[24]

By 1900, armed resistance had ground to a halt, and the struggle shifted to political activism in the form of Algerian nationalism.

THE NATIONALIST PERIOD

Algerian nationalism was born in the period prior to the First World War. It started with the *évolués* or *Young Algerians*, French-educated Algerians, who were around Emir Khaled, the grandson of Emir Abdelkader. Unlike the Tunisian and Moroccan varieties, Algerian nationalism was born abroad, in France, or to be more precise, within French communist circles. This ensured that Algerian nationalism would gradually move away from its Arab-Islamic origins towards secularization during the war of liberation and this, in turn, led to the dominance of Marxism and French culture, language, and values after independence. Later Alfred Grosser, a professor of politics, remarked that during the war of liberation, the French Government preferred to deal with the nationalists in the Maghreb rather than with their elders who 'often spoke bad French'. Grosser explained:

> The nationalists mastered French much better than Arabic, whereas their clothing and their behaviour demonstrated to what extent they had undergone the influence of our universities and of western civilization as a whole.[25]

The fact that Algerian nationalism was born in alien surroundings rather than in its own homeland, was perhaps an unavoidable historical fact. Poverty at home compelled young Algerians to emigrate to Tunisia, Morocco, and France in quest of a living. It was the French atmosphere (maltreatment and disrespect of 'inferior' Muslim immigrants, contrasting with the Leftists' humanistic solidarity with the immigrants as a 'proletariat') which made them aware of their condition and impelled them to engage in political activity in a favourable climate. The French-based nationalists, therefore, adopted the organizational structures, objectives, and even the vision of the host country's political and trade union activists. Mohamed Harbi, founder in 1968 of PAGS (which replaced the Algerian Communist Party), makes the following comment:

> The migratory movements had a considerable influence at the social and political level. The idea of nation became accessible. The people replaced the tribe, the party the religious brotherhood.[26]

This explains further the circumstances in which Algerian secularism and Marxism appeared on the Algerian scene to later impose on a Muslim people models and values alien to its civilization.

Algerian nationalism included two trends: one reformist and one revolutionary. The revolutionary tendency started with the setting up in France in 1923 of *l'Étoile Nord Africaine* (ENA, the North African Star), which was close to the French Communist Party (PCF). Its founder, Messali Hadj, a traditional Muslim, soon distanced ENA from the French communists, realizing that his objectives and views were not compatible with those of the French. From the start Messali set independence as the target of his party's political struggle and started a campaign aimed at raising the Algerian people's awareness of the necessity to put an end to its enslavement. Messali showed keen political maturity, as he, unlike the reformists, never believed that the French would eventually accept the Algerians as their equals; thus, he was to become Algeria's most appealing and charismatic nationalist leader, as all the nationalist figures still living would attest. After the banning of ENA in January 1937,[27] Messali founded in Paris almost two months later the *Parti du Peuple Algérien* (PPA) which became clandestine in 1939 and would take official, legal cover in 1946 under the name of *Mouvement pour le Triomphe des Libertés Démocratiques* (MTLD) to enable its candidates to take part in the French legislative elections of that year.

On the reformist side, there were three basic formations: the Algerian communists; *La Fédération des Élus Indigènes* (Federation of the Algerians, elected in French political and administrative institutions); and the ʿUlamāʾ Association.

The Algerian communists, recruited from the Algerian immigrant community, constituted the 'Algerian Region of the French Communist Party'. It was only in October 1936, that they became the *Algerian Communist Party* (PCA), officially autonomous vis-à-vis the French Communist Party (PCF),[28] but in reality they followed, throughout the nationalist period, to the letter the policy of the French communists who themselves were subservient to Stalin as the mentor of all the communist parties worldwide. Whenever Stalin, for the sake of Soviet national interests, changed his views, the Algerian communists did likewise. When Stalin needed an alliance with France against Germany, and consequently abandoned the idea of independence for Third World colonized countries, the Algerian communists obeyed the directives of the PCF and turned against the idea of Algeria's independence, becoming more virulent in its attacks, especially on the occasion of the 8th May 1945 massacre.[29] Later, when the Front of National Liberation (FLN) was created to start the independence struggle, they were ordered not to join it. However, in 1956, with sympathizers already in the FLN, they did join it.

The second reformist movement, *La Fédération des Élus* was founded in 1927. It was the natural extension of the *Evolués* and became active in the three main cities of Algeria: Algiers, Qacentina and Wahran. It included a group of French-educated people strongly influenced by French culture, who were to be represented by Ferhat Abbas, an eloquent pharmacist. In a controversial article published in his newspaper *L'Entente* in February 1936, Abbas denied the existence of an Algerian nation. He was a reformist in that he did not believe in Algeria's independence until he revised his position with *Le Manifeste du Peuple Algérien* of February 1943 where he denounced the idea of integration. In 1955, he joined the FLN and later became one of its prominent leaders.

THE ʿULAMĀʾ ASSOCIATION

The ʿUlamāʾ Association is the third and most important reformist movement. It was created in May 1931, although the idea for such a gathering is said to have been decided by Ben Bādīs and some other *ulamā'* while in Makkah at the end of the First World War. Contrary to the nationalist movement, it was born in the homeland and had its headquarters at its club the *Nādī et-Taraqqī* (the Club of Progress) in Algiers, and was headed by Shaykh Abdelhamid Ben Bādīs, an advocate of the 19th century Muslim Nahda led by Jamāl al-Dīn al-Afghānī and Muhammad 'Abdu. Being apolitical, not only did the *ulamā'* not capitalize on this advantage, but made serious political mistakes out of naïvety. The *Association's* statutes specify that it was set up as an 'association of moral education' aiming 'to fight social scourges' like alcoholism, gambling, and ignorance and all things 'prohibited by the [Islamic] religion' and other things 'illegal under the [French] laws and decrees in force.' Moreover Article 3 of the Statutes indicates that 'any political discussion, as well as in fact any intervention in a political question is strictly forbidden by the Association.'[30]

Through these statutes the *ulamā'* confined themselves to strictly cultural and religious renaissance activities inspired by the *Nahda* movement. But in an unexpected move in 1936, they departed from their agenda and got involved in politics. They refused an alliance with the PPA, which was ideologically and culturally close to them, and preferred to join Ferhat Abbas and the Algerian communists in calling for Algeria's integration with France. This was expressed in the 1936 Muslim Congress. This paradoxical stand earned them much criticism at a time when the other nationalist tendency (ENA-PPA-MTLD) struggled for outright independence. In view of the harsh destitution and dismal moral and religious condition to which the Algerian people were reduced, the *ulamā'* thought that by opting for integration with France, the Muslims would have the same rights as the French themselves and, as a result, they would obtain legal cover to protect the Algerians' badly dented identity and regenerate their Islamic personality. For the nationalists, this was a fallacy. The famous Muslim thinker Malek Bennabi did not spare the *ulamā'*, when he remarked in 1970:

The ʿUlamāʾ ... implicitly and unwittingly exchanged the policy that would impose on the colonial Administration the qualifying round ... for a policy of claims which gave colonialism a respite and left the initiative to it ... Therefore, when, in 1936, the ʿUlamāʾ surrendered our cultural universe to the power of the idol, this was but the march backward, the return to darkness.[31]

In any case the *ulamā* realized their mistake and reversed their position.[32] They returned to their work of ideological awareness and joined the mainstream national movement at the end of the 1930s. Their task was more strategic since it aimed to reactivate the Muslim cultural renaissance and put an end to the colonial drive to depersonalize the Algerians. Roger Garaudy, who met the second leader of the *Ulamā* Association, Shaykh al-Bashīr al-Ibrāhīmī, says in his *Testament philosophique*:

Shaykh Ibrahimi was, with Shaykh Ben Badis, the soul of a veritable 'cultural renovation' in Algeria, which made possible the liberation of the Algerian people, in 1962, from 130 years of alienation, and the recovery of its Arab-Islamic identity for which his people have never ceased to struggle, from Abd-el-Qader's resistance to the insurrections of Shaykh Bouamama and of el-Moqrani, to the 1954 uprising and to the liberating victory of 1962.[33]

For the *ulamā* the question of the struggle for independence could not be tackled in all its aspects without the framework of Islam. For them the point was not to aim at Algeria's independence simply to replace the colonial administration with Algerian rulers who would exercise authority using the same colonialist laws – which is exactly what happened after independence and has led to the present tragedy. Their main concern was, in Garaudy's terms,

to create a new community, based on values radically different from those which had been imposed, for 130 years, by the occupying power: specifically Islamic values.[34]

Their programme was, therefore, a real cultural revolution which aimed at changing man and thus paving the ideological way for the war of liberation. The task was an immense priority and may provide a reason for their political naïvety and slips. Explaining their programme, Garaudy says:

> ... the men who created with Shaykh Ben Badis and Shaykh Ibrahimi, the 'Ulamā' Association in 1931, put at the top of their programme a gigantic effort in education, against depersonalization by the colonialist power which was attempting to uproot the Algerian child from his Arab-Islamic culture, as well as against the obscurantism of the marabouts which, with its superstitions and its 'intercessions', was so contrary to the spirit of Islam (and was, for this reason, cherished by the colonialist authorities).[35]

With the massacre of nearly 50,000 Algerians between 8-15 May 1945,[36] a repression made all the more bitter inasmuch as the Algerians had just sacrificed a few hundred thousand of their best soldiers on the German front for the sake of France,[37] ended up uniting the *'ulamā'*, the *Élus*, and the nationalists in a broad national movement that was to lead to the war of liberation in 1954.

THE WAR OF LIBERATION: 1954-1962

The war of liberation, called 'the Algerian revolution', was the outcome of various forces led by the members of the nationalist PPA-MTLD who set up the Front of National Liberation (FLN) and the Army of National Liberation (ALN). The FLN required that all the former parties' members join it individually in order to give it a real cohesion, the form of a new party rather than a coalition. Its political charter released on 1st November, at the beginning of the almost eight-year struggle, stipulates in article 2 that the struggle aimed to achieve independence through 'the re-establishment of the social, democratic, sovereign Algerian state within the framework of Islamic principles.'[38]

Although the formulation of the Islamic orientation of the struggle was vague enough to lend itself to future interpretation, in the early years of the war of liberation, the FLN insisted on 'Religious belonging as the cement of national unity, [with] Islam understood not only as a culture, but as the foundation of society and of political unity, governing what is public and what is private without distinction.'[39] The Islamic coloration of the struggle was evident, then, in the very terminology used: it was a matter of *jihād*, the fighters were *mujāhidīn* and the organic structure of the FLN was known as the *Nidham*;[40] the discipline enforced by the *Nidham* among the *mujāhidīn* and the Algerian people at large was largely inspired by Islamic teachings: prohibition of alcohol and gambling, enforcement of the Islamic moral code in society and the practice of all essential religious obligations. These were to continue until independence in 1962. The FLN's Islamic discourse showed that Algeria belonged to a different cultural sphere.

However, the inclusion of the Algerian question, for the first time, on the United Nations' agenda in September 1955, marked the beginning of the FLN's ideological shift. Anxious to court the western nations the FLN was henceforth to adopt 'a cautious ambiguity',[41] using an increasingly secular discourse while referring to its Arab-Islamic background.

In August 1956, a meeting of the FLN and ALN's internal and external leadership, called the Soummam Conference, consecrated this trend under the influence of new Marxist elements. The Conference adopted a new political platform through which it clearly distanced itself from Islam as an ideological base in favour of the more vague Arab-Islamic concept. Islam was thereby reduced 'by the new FLN ideologues to a moral effort [which] did not reflect popular convictions, thus erasing an important dimension of a "specificity" which was otherwise constantly claimed.'[42] Malek Bennabi calls this new double discourse the FLN's 'bilingualism' phenomenon and sums it up cogently:

> In reality, its [the phenomenon's] consequences started manifesting themselves since 1956 ... they began taking shape in a debate concerning the very terminology of the revolution itself. Certain terms were being discussed so that they could be replaced by new ones. The people started speaking more and more about the *jundi* [soldier] who had earlier been *al-Mujahid*. The debate went beyond the terminology to include the structures themselves. Consequently, the *Nidham* disappeared to be replaced by prefabricated structures whose baptism was taken care of in the Soummam Conference. Thus, there

came into existence the "Executive Committee" and the "National Council of the Algerian Revolution".[43]

The Algerian Communist Party identified with this secularization phenomenon and so joined the FLN in 1956, which was to reinforce further the new trend of the FLN and pave the way for a secular Algerian state at independence. Tawfīq al-Shāwī, a former professor of international relations at Cairo University and now director of the Arabic weekly *Al-Mujtama'*, reveals another interesting aspect confirming the link between the trend towards secularization trend and the emergence of a French role:

'France agreed on [the principle of] independence after satisfying itself that authority in Algeria would be assumed by nationalists[44] who had forsaken the Algerian struggle's requirement of establishing an Islamic state.' This is because 'taking away the Islamic content of national independence is a strategic objective for colonialist powers.'[45]

Algeria acceded to political independence in July 1962 and the FLN became the ruling party under a one-party system. But, because they did not have a clear Islamic vision and programme, the Algerian nationalists, including those who were and are sincere believers, opened the door to the predominance in Algeria after independence of secularism, Marxism, the recolonization of Algerian society by France in a different way, and even the persecution of the *'ulamā'* and all those adhering to an Islamic project for Algeria.[46] In fact many of the traditional Muslim nationalist politicians, like Benyoucef Ben Khedda and Ferhat Abbas, were marginalized, while some others like Ben Bella flirted with Marxist ideology and were also swept aside by a more radical, French-educated and Marxist-oriented new class of politicians who took the country's destiny in their hands and fashioned a new francophile elite in their image, the elite which was to be dubbed *Hizb Fransa* by the rising Islamic movement in the early 1980s.

While Marxism was to become the new regime's economic and social project – at least in theory – in practice, French language, culture, and way of life were to become the norm and achieve, as *non-material* institutions, what France had never been able to achieve with its antagonistic, *physical* presence in the country. Henceforth, French language, culture, and values were to become the invisible, mostly undeclared, but ever present motives underlying France's relations with independent Algeria47 and France was to defend her presence in Algerian society with all the necessary means. It is therefore extremely important to bear these facts in mind if one wishes to understand the hidden roots of the present oppression of the Algerian people.

Perhaps the best summary of France's presence in post-independence Algeria was given by an Algerian poet – an Arabic-speaking poet – who is currently spending his last years in an old people's home. *Kharajtī, Firansa, wa lam takhrujī, fa bismi ta'awwuninā kharibtī*: 'O France! You have left [Algeria], but in reality you have not; for in the name of cooperation you undermine.'

ALGERIAN-FRENCH RELATIONS: 1962-1996

Algeria offers a unique case whereby the resistance to French domination, through the popular expression of Islam, was judged to be so alarming48 that even truly free elections were foiled, with *French* assistance, by the Algerian francophile military caste. The point was for France to maintain Algeria under its influence through the corruption of army and civilian leaders even if this were to lead to a bloodbath. The official French line is that France does not interfere in Algeria's internal affairs. Lucile Provost takes an opposing view in this respect, saying that France's official non-intervention is but a smoke screen concealing 'other motives first related to the support for the Algerian authorities, but more deeply, perhaps, linked to the [French] refusal to accept Algerian society in its reality.'49

Algerian-French relations have gone through three stages corresponding to major events in Algeria, which brought about a change of direction: The Ben Bella-Boumediènne 'nationalist' period (1962-1980); the Chadli Bendjedid period (1980-1988) of so-called economic liberalization which led to a total dependence of Algeria on France and on the major western financial institutions; finally, the period of forced political liberalization brought about by the Algerian people's pressure for change – a change forced on the traditional army-dominated regime by the sudden entry of the Islamic movement into the political field, which led the army leaders and the *Ḥizb Fransa* to seize power once more (1988-1996).

Algeria became officially independent on 5th July 1962 under the Évian Agreements. The FLN was imposed as the ruling party in a one-party system, with a socialist orientation. The few old *'ulamā'* and Muslim intellectuals who survived the war of liberation, and were kept out of the political field, were alarmed by the socialist slogans. They thought that Algerian society was moving out of the French frying pan into the Marxist fire.[50] France had left physically but had remained as a concept in spite of the nominally independent policy of Algeria towards France, and despite all the vicissitudes of the two countries' relations.

Indeed, there was no clear-cut severance between Algeria and France and this was at the insistence of Paris.[51] This insistence, as well as the privileged relations France wanted to have with the new state through substantial financial aid[52] were, at the economic level, motivated by the presence of oil and other minerals in Algerian soil. On the one hand, nearly one million French settlers (called *Pieds Noirs*) left Algeria for good; on the other hand thousands of French technical assistants arrived in Algeria to work in all fields, not least of all, education.

In overtly political terms, the French may have gone, but their hold on the country remained and was reinforced in different ways. This was to lead to a triple domination of Algeria: economically, culturally, and politically.

ECONOMIC DOMINATION

Algeria has been a very lucrative market for French business. French banks and industries admit to having earned substantial profits there.[53] It is important to understand that France has maintained its economic, political, and cultural influence in Algeria through the corruption of the francophile oligarchy of Algerian civilian and military elites, which has had no scruples in plundering its country's wealth. A key French official involved in Algeria's affairs in French political and espionage circles is quoted thus:

> [In Algeria] power was – and still is – in the hands of a few clans which loot their country and share between themselves gigantic commissions, which, from a cynical and practical point of view, made things easier for us [the French] who had the opportunity to win a number of, say, active sympathisers.[54]

Many of those who have held the highest posts in the Algerian army and who positioned their family and clan members in key political and economic posts had served as non-commissioned officers in the French army; they joined the Army of National Liberation (ALN) shortly before Algeria's independence, and this has always been interpreted by Algerian public opinion, as well as by some upright personalities, as a French strategy of positioning its own men in the new state's machinery from its inception. This view is supported by the transfer from Morocco in 1962 of 5,000 Algerians who had undergone intensive training by French experts to enable them to take over the Algerian administration from the French. Meanwhile, a law on external trade issued in 1971 which banned intermediaries between the Algerian state and its suppliers was seen as a way of institutionalizing corruption and keeping it within a small and mainly military caste, supposedly far from the public eye.[55]

Moreover, to conceal their secret dealings with the French that were contrary to the national interests of Algeria, the new clique resorted to official anti-French rhetoric at regular intervals, at a time when France was slowly but surely cultivating candidates for corruption and building up its various civilian and military networks of informers and collaborators.[56] These networks still exist today. The fact that 'within the most closed circles of the authorities some economic or political officials are [Algerian-French] binationals' indicates the extent of the corruption networks. Very revealing, too, is 'the rule [which] is naturally to conceal this double nationality.' So shocking are these facts to any Algerian with self-respect that Lucile Provost, a former official of the French Foreign Ministry, confessed that such facts were a surprise to her 'Cartesian mind'.[57] For their part, the French have engaged in 'all sorts of secret dishonest dealings'[58] with the Algerian rulers without any scruples throughout the last thirty-four years of 'independent' Algeria in order to keep the country under their influence.

Post-independence Algerian-French relations started, under President Ben Bella's nationalistic policy, with a spate of nationalizations of French interests which began as soon as October 1962 with small factories and services. After the 5th June 1965 coup which brought Colonel Houari Boumediènne to power, nationalizations affected the mining and steel industries, the banking system, as well as the distribution network of oil products.

Yet French companies continued to operate at least until the beginning of the 1970s in spite of Boumediènne's apparently hardline socialism. They remained in place in such fields as construction, automobiles, pharmaceuticals, and hydrocarbons, which were both lucrative and safe from nationalization. An agreement in July 1965 gave France a dominant position in the exploitation of the Algerian hydrocarbon market until 1971 when the hydrocarbons sector was nationalized entirely. Furthermore, between 1967 and 1978 six French firms won 50% of industrial equipment contracts and the same proportion of infrastructure equipment, while in the field of hydrocarbons, France obtained one third of the contracts.[59]

The continuance of French companies in Algeria, in the face of the apparently harsh socialist odds, was not without reason. The fact is that the presence at the head of Algeria of a politico-military 'mafia', greedy for commissions has made the task of French industrialists and officials easy. Dr. Abdelhamid Brahimi, former planning minister and prime minister, gives three telling examples[60] of the major areas of corruption. Algeria's pharmaceutical needs have been an exclusive French monopoly since independence. The medicines are often out of date and bought at prices much higher than normal international rates, a fact which no French source has mentioned so far. Between 1970 and 1994, there had been a number of corruption scandals involving French companies and others, which were quickly covered up. In the field of pharmaceuticals Algeria's loss was two-fold: not only did it have to bear the chronic overpricing of each imported product resulting from the commissions taken by the Algerian officials, but also the large quantities of outdated medicines that were bought, and had to be destroyed, were never replaced by the French suppliers. French red meat is bought at prices twice and even three times higher than those charged by African countries, while wheat is bought at prices up to and even over 30% above the market price, as a result of the combined effect of an overcharge on grain and high credit terms. Today, one third of total Algerian imports originate from France, compared with 17%-18% in the 1980s. These major areas are quasi-monopolies of French companies. Mostly in focus is the case of the pharmaceuticals: according to a source in the United States, an American company made an offer to some Algerian officials to supply medicines to Algeria in bulk and below the market price, in addition to building a factory for the production of packaging. The offer was reportedly turned down because the Algerian party argued that the consignments would have to go via France for commissions that had to be paid there. Similarly, a pharmaceutical complex built in Algeria in the mid-1980s is reportedly still idle because of the pressure to import medicines from France where a commission-based deal appears to be binding on the Algerian business clique.

The French companies which had left under the pressure of Boumedienne's nationalizations, had nevertheless kept in touch with the country and reinforced their presence after Colonel Chadli Bendjedid's takeover in 1979. With Bendjedid at the helm, Algeria was to slump from 1980 onwards into a state of renewed dependency upon France and upon the international money lenders, along with the inevitable spread of corruption this entailed.

A French industrialist is reported to have said in this respect: 'I have never seen a *nomenklatura* so greedy and with so little concern for its country's interests. At a certain time, the official in charge of the *Office algérien des céréales* [wheat import state organization] – this is not an isolated case – demanded a 25% commission from his western negotiators instead of the traditional 2%. That was tantamount to looting.'61 In her book, Lucile Provost mentions the establishment of 'veritable networks of political-economic influence with the former colonial power and which still exist today'.[62]

CULTURAL DOMINATION

The economic domination of Algeria by France went hand in hand with and strengthened the now well-known French 'cultural diplomacy' which aimed at securing cultural influence/hegemony in former colonies through all possible means. 'Cultural cooperation' meant purely and simply a one-way French cultural domination of independent Algeria, which was ensured basically in the Évian Agreements.[63] So, at independence in 1962, the point for France was to succeed in making of Algeria the bastion of *francophonie*, which explains why a great part of its foreign ministry cultural cooperation budget has been devoted to Algeria.[64] Such a policy could not be implemented without a strategy designed to choke Arab-Islamic cultural endeavours, which was to be facilitated by several factors.

The considerable influx of French *cooperants techniques* did play a great part in firmly establishing French cultural presence. But the Algerian administrative, political, and military francophile lobbies, which held the decision-making levers within the new state, paved the way for it through a series of 'strategic' measures. The Marxist orientation of the regime, with its secularist, anti-religious slant, contributed to French cultural designs. The few schools of the *'Ulamā' Association* were closed down immediately after independence under the pretext that education was a state monopoly.[65] In the meantime, the country was open to French socio-cultural influences in the form of music, fashion, cinema, and all kinds of literature which conveyed theories, ideas, values, social attitudes, and sensitivities that were and are fundamentally alien and mainly antagonistic to the Islamic character of Algerian society. With the severe state control and monopoly on the import of books and other literature, in favour of all that was French, the mechanisms of a one-way social interaction were firmly established. The door was thus forcibly closed to Islamic culture which was not allowed to develop *organically* on its own ground. This represented a subtle cultural oppression which the ordinary man would take time to notice.[66]

French books filled the libraries and bookshops of Algeria when Arabic books were still rare in the first decade of independence, and of poor quality. Arabic books subsequently imported from the Middle East were subject to severe censorship. For example, the late thinker Malek Bennabi produced over twenty books mainly in French, all of which were translated into Arabic. None, except one of an autobiographical/historical nature, have been printed in Algeria by the state publishing company SNED (later ENAL) or were even imported by it, to this day. Bennabi himself was silenced and later persecuted for holding 'reactionary' ideas.[67] Also, when some ʿulamāʾ wanted to publish their views in defence of Islam in the face of the post-independence Marxist ideological and French cultural onslaught, they had to do it in Morocco,[68] whose authorities allowed this only because of their dispute with Algeria over the Western Sahara.

The francophiles were the only ones to be published either at home or in France. Thus the intellectual debate was a one-way, secular, francophone, 'modernist' debate with hardly any exception. This, with the massive influx of various forms of French culture, gradually fashioned the tastes, sensitivities, and ideas of the generation of independence. A good many elements of this generation were to constitute the French lobby or the intellectual part of the *Hizb Fransa*.

Education was in French. In the year of independence, Arabic was a 'foreign language' on the same footing as English, German, or Spanish. It was not until the following year (1963-1964), that Arabic became the 'national language', although without being given the means to compete with French. The process of the arabization of education, initiated by the then President Ben Bella under the influence of an Arab nationalist trend within the new state machinery, was slow and was carried out with hastily recruited Egyptian teachers, most of whom were apparently not qualified. After the 1965 coup, the new president Boumediènne, Arabic-speaking himself, made arabization a target to be achieved in education and in the administration. The arabization of education did make considerable headway because this was a political decision by Boumediènne; however the arabization of administration and of the government machinery made hardly any progress due to the resistance of an essentially francophone civil servant corps.

In the meantime, in the mid-1960s, a campaign was launched which aimed at raising Algerian colloquial Arabic to the level of a national language, with French as the language of science and development. Standard Arabic as the only written Arabic and also as the language of the Qur'ān, was dubbed 'alien' to Algerian society – especially by Berber francophile activists – or at best inadequate to express modern knowledge and science as effectively as French. Although this campaign did not have much impact, in spite of the production of some plays and literary pieces, it nevertheless acted as one of the safeguards of French language and culture, helping to maintain their supremacy in everyday life, and served also as a means of gaining access to the best positions available in the field of employment.

In the 1980s, the arabization of education eventually reached higher education, but still without much effect on the French cultural and linguistic hegemony. Yet, the French saw this as a turning point for the status of their linguistic and cultural dominance.[69] In the absence of scientific studies in this field, various facts taken together show that the French were, behind the scenes, doing their best to preserve this dominance, while their journalists, intellectuals, and officials, have criticized arabization as a 'humiliation' for them and have seen it as a threat to *francophonie*.[70]

In 1988, the then Algerian Education Minister naively dared to call for the replacement of French in schools by English – and was sacked immediately.[71] When, in 1989, under the pressure of the now very popular Islamic Salvation Front (FIS), the ruling FLN party adopted a bill aimed at seriously generalizing arabization, the French socialists in power did take it seriously (this time due to the presence in the political field of the Islamic movement). Premier Michel Rocard called on the Algerian francophile *Hizb Fransa* 'to save the French language'[72] and a pro-French demonstration mainly by Berberists took place. When the bill was to become law, in July 1992 – that is, six months after the coup – it was postponed indefinitely. The influence of French culture was such that Mohamed Boudiaf, a francophone former nationalist leader, who was brought from his Moroccan exile by the leaders of the 1992 coup to head the country on their behalf, declared to the French daily, *Le Monde*, regarding arabization:

> All this is demagogy. However, the problem is that there is a pro-Arab sensitivity at the level of national education, something very artificial. Arabic, Islam, national values are often referred to, but we shall go beyond them.[73]

Not content with their leverage at the economic and political levels, the French made efforts under President Chadli Bendjedid's rule to influence the educational system which they rightly consider to be strategic in the long run, and which had already been arabized to a great extent. Attempts were made at two levels: a) discrimination against Muslim students in the granting of joint French-Algerian 'co-operation' scholarships (60% French, 40% Algerian); b) efforts to put Algerian educational curricula under their own influence and to discourage the arabization of education. The following details are very significant. [74]

De-selecting of candidates: In matters of joint cooperation scholarships, which were in force in 1989/1990, the French had normally no role in the selection of the candidates for the scholarships, except for a right to check the candidates' linguistic standard. Yet, in reality, French educational representatives would interview the candidates and ask about their religious commitment and political affiliation (the Islamic FIS had just been set up and was the most popular political party in the country). Candidates who showed exterior signs of Islamic commitment (beards for men, headscarves for women, for example) or sympathy with FIS were automatically de-selected. Thus, candidates brilliant in mathematics, already selected on the Algerian side for postgraduate studies in France, were dropped as a result of French interference.

Influencing the curriculum: In an attempt to put the Algerian higher educational system under their control, the French despatched the

President of *École Centrale* to try to persuade the Algerian higher educational authorities to align their mathematics curriculum with the French one. He is reported to have argued that Morocco had already accepted the principle and that Tunisia was on the way to doing so. The idea was that Algerian students would do two preparatory years in an Algerian university, then have a full B.Sc. course in a French university. The aim was twofold: on the one hand the French realized that most of those Algerian students who had trained in French universities were committed to Islam, worked very hard, and did return to Algeria where they took up influential positions. By controlling the undergraduate curriculum, the French would ensure that such positions would fall to francophile, secularized Algerian graduates who would secure Algeria's techno-logical dependence on France. On the other hand, by training selected, secular-minded Algerian students according to French technological needs, the French could tempt them to join their academic research world, which has been deserted by French graduates in favour of the more lucrative private business sector. It is undeniable that today in France, North Africans do fill a sizeable portion of French scientific research posts – albeit at the junior level.

In the meantime, during a visit to a key Algerian scientific university in 1990, M. Feuvret, Director of the famous French *École des Arts et Métiers*, lobbied against the on-going arabization of education, arguing that Algeria needed a *scientific* language for its technological development and that Arabic was not up to it. He is reported to have been irritated when some Algerian academics cited the Japanese technological advance obtained through the medium of their own language, and when it was argued that many French researchers resort to English to publish their research works.

Obviously, arabization was not seen by France as a mere exchange of one language with another one, but as the vehicle of an underlying civilizational project which was to be undermined by any means. So along with this discreet type of lobbying, other anti-Islamic means were resorted to. A case in point was that of a university member of staff who along with his wife was severely burnt by the explosion of a gas bottle. Separately, his wife obtained a visa for immediate treatment in France; but when the man was seen with a beard (in a photograph), the French consulate refused to grant him a visa. When it was argued that his wife had already obtained a visa, hers was cancelled and was only renewed through high-level intervention in Algiers. In the meantime the husband died of his burns.[75]

POLITICAL DOMINATION

In her recent book, Lucile Provost referred to the strongly reaffirmed 'sacrosanct principle of [French] non-interference' in Algerian affairs, explaining that in fact

it hides other motives first of all connected with its assistance to the Algerian authorities, but also, perhaps more profoundly, linked to the [French] refusal to accept Algerian society as it is. Of Algeria, France seems to recognise only that which is French, or seems to be so, or feigns to be so.[76]

This illustrates how from the beginning the French have made a principle, not of non-interference, but of undermining the Algerian Islamic movement simply because Islam is and remains that which is considered to be *the* obstacle to France's *mission civilisatrice*. Very few observers have noted that *Hizb Fransa*, or the 'eradicators', have become bold in opposing the Algerian people's will for change and freedom for one key reason, namely, because *Hizb Fransa* is supported by the French government.[77]

1988 was a turning point in France's relations with Algeria. That year coincided with the sudden, unprecedented political expression of the Algerian Islamic movement. Henceforth, on the one hand, France was to devote all its energies to operate the classical scenario, namely, to use its now strong base and contacts in Algeria so as to push its Algerian military pawns to the pinnacles of power and consolidate their grip; on the other, it was to devote much effort in devising and implementing a strategy aimed at undermining the Islamic movement which was to be 'assimilated to Nazism'.[78] From then on, parts of the French political, intellectual, and media establishments – including strong well-known Zionist elements – have given to their opposition to Islam and its representative movements the form of a crusade. French-Algerian relations were to focus essentially on systematically distorting the aims of the Islamic Front (FIS) and presenting it as anti-western, while leading a diplomatic campaign against its members in Europe and America.

The French socialists, in power, were the first to show publicly their anti-Islamism after the massacre of about 1,300 young demonstrators in Algiers between the 5th and 10th of October 1988.[79] President Mitterrand rushed immediate aid consignments to keep the threatened Algerian regime afloat while his Prime Minister Michel Rocard knew 'how to find the phrases which avoid condemning the repression too openly'.[80] In the meantime, all the European parties in power 'diplomatically' condemned the massacre, except the French socialists. Nearly a month later, in November, the French Socialist Parliamentary Group leader justified, in a BBC World Service news bulletin, his party's silence over the Algerian massacre, saying: 'We did not condemn it as we were waiting to find out whether the Islamists were behind it; this is because we will never allow the emergence of an Islamic republic in Algeria.'

The setting up of the Islamic Salvation Front (FIS) in March 1989, its subsequent legalization, and above all its unprecedented popularity in the history of independent Algeria caused quite a stir in Paris. From now on a whole machinery, secret and open, was to be set in motion to frustrate the will of the Algerian people to choose Islam as the basis of their political life.

The Algerian generals – the core of whom were former French army non-commissioned officers who promoted to their rank other francophile elements – now openly in power, swore 'to turn Algeria into a lake of blood'[81] if the FIS came to power. Meanwhile, French Premier Michel Rocard advised his newly elected Algerian counterpart Mouloud Hamrouche on an electoral strategy, 'made in Paris' and designed to deprive the Islamic movement of any chances of winning elections.[82] When the municipal elections were held in June 1990 and resulted in the overwhelming victory of the Islamic Front, with the FIS leadership's pressuring the Algerian President for new legislative elections, French officials urged President Chadli Bendjedid not to dissolve the National People's Assembly.[83] Bendjedid fixed the date of the forthcoming legislative elections but not before putting behind bars the FIS leadership amidst a francophile media war unleashed against FIS. During the legislative elections campaign, the EEC interfered in the campaign with an official statement, issued conspicuously under French influence, to condemn FIS, while French officials and MPs intervened by making public declarations hostile to the Islamic party.[84] When FIS once again obtained a resounding victory, far ahead of the two other main parties (FFS and FLN), the French media relayed the Algerian francophile media's own campaign to press for a coup against FIS.[85]

There have been hints in the French press that France may have been behind the Algerian generals' coup.[86] In fact, reliable sources in the Algerian government of the time disclosed that Algerian Interior Minister General Larbi Belkheir, who was on a mission to the Élysée on 10th January 1992, confided to an Algerian colleague that from the following day 'the Islamists will not be seen in the streets any longer.'[87] The repression that ensued was to lead to a bloodbath, with the active assistance of France.

French support for the new illegitimate military authorities in their fight against the Islamic movement was very quick.[88] The French embarked on consolidating the new rulers by supplying them with military counter-insurgency equipment. In the meantime *Le Berry* a French spy ship equipped with sophisticated electronic listening devices have since patrolled the Algerian coastline listening to inter-garrison and government telephone communications, while French radar planes as well as the French-Spanish-Italian satellite Hélios[89] daily gather detailed data to prevent a possible counter-coup by 'nationalist' officers.

On the economic front, France has been keeping the generals afloat through French 'aid' as well as aid from the international financial institutions. Therefore, since the 1992 coup the country has been completely at France's mercy.

In the West, Paris embarked on a policy designed to silence any

Islamic voice likely to oppose the protected generals. In France five pro-FIS pamphlets were officially banned, and many Muslims have been intimidated, while proven FIS supporters were rounded up and sent to Ouagadougou or have been languishing in French jails, with their families discreetly starved through the withdrawal of benefits. In Europe Paris evokes the spectre of 'terrorism' to exercise diplomatic pressure on Britain and other countries of the European Community in order to obtain the silencing of Algerian nationals giving interviews or issuing publications like the weeklies *Al-Tabṣira* and *Al-Anṣār*. In Belgium it obtained the imprisonment of seven prominent FIS members, one of whom, Shaykh Ahmed al-Zawi, is an elected FIS member of parliament. Dr. Said Lahlali, a FIS MP initially expelled to Switzerland by the French police, was handed over *manu militari* in early 1996 to the French authorities by Geneva, at the insistence of Paris, because he was making representations to UN human rights committees over the concentration camps and large-scale killings in Algeria.

On 21st January 1995, on the initiative of the indefatigably anti-immigrant and anti-Islamic French Interior Minister Charles Pasqua, the countries of the Maghreb (excluding Morocco) and France, Italy, Spain, and Portugal met in Tunisia to discuss ways and means to eradicate the Islamic movement in the Maghreb. In the Tunis Declaration they assimilated the Islamic movement to 'criminal' and 'terrorist' organizations. Most noticeable was the Declaration's insistence on the 'common will to use all means to preserve the innumerable ties between the two sides of the Mediterranean',[90] which shows once again that France has strong vested interests in the region and sees the Islamist movement as an obstacle to its designs in the Maghreb.

Furthermore, observers widely acknowledge that the 16th November 1995 presidential elections which brought General Khaled Nezzar back to power were the work of Paris officials, who advised the Algerian generals to acquire a façade of legitimacy which would give France and the West in general a pretext for dealing more openly and freely with the Algerian junta.

THE FRENCH MEDIA ESTABLISHMENT

The French media establishment has played a vanguard role, fully mobilized for France's anti-Islamic agenda, distorting the identity and objectives of the Algerian Islamic movement.[91] The aim was both to confuse the Algerian people at large and the francophone – and *a fortiori*, francophile – and otherwise 'neutral' cadres. Conditioning further western – even Muslim – public opinion against Algerian Islamists was also a prime goal, thus paving the way for any future interventions.

Since the October 1988 popular uprising in particular, much of the French media thus engaged in a campaign of disinformation regarding Algeria. A case in point is a statement by the late Mohamed Saïd.[92] In June 1990, after the FIS victory at the local elections, he addressed the Algerians advising them to get ready to 'change their food and clothing habits', which in the Algerian context meant that the wasting of food and purchase of expensive imported clothes, to the detriment of local production, would have to be discarded if Algeria were really to become self-sufficient and develop. The French media – and behind it the other western press which take it as a source – reported that Mohamed Saïd was warning that the Algerians would henceforth have to eat on the floor and without cutlery, as opposed to eating around tables, and to discard western-style clothes in favour of the national garment, the *Jellaba*.

When the armed resistance to the cancellation of the elections started, most of the atrocities, committed by the Algerian security services in disguise[93] and blamed by the Algerian junta on 'Islamic terrorism' were widely reported by the French media.[94] On the other hand, it has actively blacked out the voices of those who were victorious in the ballots and gave prominence to francophile elements alienated from their people's values and language, which made Burgat say:

> The few empty acronyms brandished [during the two successive ballots] by a small number of political communication specialists were, indeed, to have at their disposal in France, a media coverage in inverse proportion to the reality of their social anchorage in Algeria. In

too great a part of the French intelligentsia, disinformation was thus to have long-lasting ravages, and the psychological war initiated by the Algerian secret services was to register impressive successes.95

In this way, the massacre in their cells of over three hundred Muslim prisoners in the Berrouagia jail in November 1994, west of the capital city, and of one hundred and four other Muslims in the notorious Serkaji prison in Algiers itself on 21st February 1995, was blacked out. In the meantime, the conspicuous promotion of francophile officials and intellectuals has been aired on prime-time French television programmes, and given prominence in the written press and publishing world.

CONCLUSION

The resounding victory of the FIS in the June 1990 local elections, gave food for thought to France's ambassador in Algiers. He seemed to have drawn the lesson from the massive vote in favour of an Islamic party, a vote which followed nearly thirty years of Marxist orientation in the political culture of the Algerian elites. In an open letter addressing the French Government, published in the French daily *Le Monde* shortly after the elections, the ambassador argued that Algerian society had shown that it had a set of values, languages, and a civilization that were all radically different from those of France and that the latter had to review its policies towards the whole Maghreb if it did not want to lose this part of the world to the English and the Americans. But the socialist President Mitterrand, who had already chosen to throw all the might of the French government behind the new military regime, did not heed such an view.

France, as a post-colonialist power, has always built its foreign relations on hegemony – cultural first, political and economic afterwards. The only thing that has changed since the era of colonialism is subtlety, or what one could call in modern terms the *packaging* of its policies towards the societies formerly under its rule. This is the case not only in Algeria, but also in France's other former colonies in Africa. In each of its former colonies, it invariably left a francophile elite and/or a dictator in command. When these dictators and the overt French domination are rejected by African peoples, French troops and a squadron of planes stationed locally are moved from one place to another to nip any revolt in the bud. The examples abound from Chad to Zaire, Central Africa to Rwanda and the Ivory Coast.[96]

Today, the French government seems to be focusing on two key objectives: the eradication of the Islamicity of Algerian society by constantly undermining its Islamic movement, and the economic domination of the Algerian people. Thus, since the 1992 coup there has been an attempt at psychologically breaking down the Algerian people through repression and disinformation over the Islamic movement's aims, with a view to disconnecting the people from the Islamic project altogether. In the meantime, through the IMF, the World Bank, and European money lenders, the country is being put in a state of near-total dependency[97] on the West, while the oil, gas, and precious mineral-rich Sahara desert has been distributed in huge concessions to western oil companies, including the French Elf-Erap and Total. This occurred immediately after the bogus presidential elections of November 1995 in Algeria – reported to have been held at the insistence of Paris which was keen to bestow upon the Algerian junta a semblance of international legitimacy.

The conflict underway in Algeria is not a civil war, but a cultural struggle between an intrinsically Islamic people and an elite which is educated in French, thinks in French, and is bent on implementing the French project of undermining Algerian society's Islamic identity.

If anything, France's *fundamentalist* anti-Islamic attitude shows that this country has not forsaken its *mission civilisatrice* which involves colonizing and imposing by force of arms its culture and language as a prelude to economic domination. Jacques Lafon, a professor at Paris University, reaffirmed this truism in 1995, during President Chirac's first visit to Britain: 'It has been a long time since conquest and cultural expansion have gone hand in hand', he pointed out.[98] The Manichean French attitude of either 'cultural domination or total rupture,' was best explained by *Politique étrangère*, a journal under the aegis of the French Prime Minister's office, in the conclusion of one of its papers. The author, a senior researcher at the

Study and Research Centre on Strategies and Technologies (CREST) of École Polytechnique in France, argued throughout his paper that Algerian-French relations in the last 30 years, have confirmed that there exists 'a true relationship which unites the two [Algerian and French] peoples, without ulterior motives in spite of the violence of the war'[99] of liberation of Algeria, and that this bond should be strengthened. However, in his conclusion, revealingly entitled 'The Future of all the Dangers', the author regrets the fact that there is an Islamically-based questioning of French cultural domination. Whether a relation can exist at all in the future between the two countries depends very much on whether the cultural specificity and the sovereignty of Algeria will be fully recognized and respected by France.

Some courageous French intellectuals and writers have come forward to press for a review of French policy towards Algeria. Apart from François Burgat, Lucile Provost has also urged:

> We, the French people, must accept the need finally to examine the twists and turns of our policy towards this country, which has somehow remained a part of ourselves, that we establish our responsibility and that of the Algerians regarding the events which hit us today, that we play vis-à-vis Algeria a role which should no longer be dictated by the ghosts of the past. This is the price to pay if France wants to envisage [a positive] outcome for this second war of Algeria.[100]

The last sentence of the quotation indicates clearly that France does have a key role in the Algerian tragedy. But France has not so far shown any sign of wishing to bring to conclusion a drama which it rather seems to intensify and perpetuate.[101] It emerges from the various statements and attitudes of French officials, intellectuals, and media that France is not about to adopt a new frame of mind on the issue. It has not questioned its blind backing of a clique of corrupt generals who have certainly created the 'lake of blood' they promised at the outset of the democratic process.[102] When the choice had to be made, the Élysée did not think twice, the constant principle of its external policy being one of hegemony – instead of the much advertized smoke screen of non-interference. Edward Said confirmed this when he said, regarding France, that, 'Though most of the colonies have won their independence, many of the imperial attitudes underlying colonial conquest continue.'[103]

The French who have themselves, since at least the 1970s, understandably developed an interesting legal arsenal to defend the French language against the invasion of English, and who in the last GATT agreements justifiably showed strong opposition to its US-dominated cultural chapter – to quote but these two examples – ought to wake up and heed the Algerian people's own demand for cultural sovereignty. 'There is no political reality if it is not supported by a cultural reality', said a French cinema commentator in October 1996, explaining that by reality she meant 'identity'.[104]

It is not too late for France to abandon its crusade-like war against Islam and its representative movements and to stop distorting its nature and aims. Some courageous voices[105] have already been making a few, small, dissenting waves in an ocean of incommensurate blindness and stubbornness. Will the voice of reason prevail?

NOTES

1. M. Faujas, *La Frontière algéro-marocaine*, Grenoble, 1906, p. 33, quoted in Ahmed el-Ammari, *Islam and the West: Historical Evolution and the Concept of Power*, London, IIIT, 1995, unpublished.

2. A complex developed due to the successive wars in which France was defeated, including the Franco-Prussian war (1870-71), World War I, World War II – a complex which was reportedly a reason for France's drive to conquer weaker countries in order to take up its position with the major powers. See 'L'intervention dans la politique étrangère de la France', in *Politique étrangère*, 1/1986, p. 176.

3. The examples of the racist motive abound, expressed by prominent military authorities and politicians, both at the time of conquest and in recent decades. See, for example, Ferhat Abbas, *Autopsie d'une guerre*, Paris: Editions Garnier, 1980, p. 222; Roger Garaudy, *Pour un dialogue des civilisations*, Paris: Denoël, 1977, p. 54.

4. Hicham Djait, *Europe and Islam: Culture and Modernity*, London:

University of California Press, 1985, pp. 34-35.

5. Ahmed Mahsas, *Le mouvement révolutionnaire en Algérie: de la 1ère guerre mondiale à 1954*, Algiers: Editions Barkat, 1990, p. 323.

6. See Roger Garaudy, *Pour un dialogue des civilisations*, op. cit., p. 56 and passim.

7. Ibid., p. 56-57.

8. See note 2 above.

9. Charles R. Ageron, *Histoire de l'Algérie contemporaine (1830-1979)*, Paris: PUF, 1980, p. 6.

10. Ahmed Mahsas, op. cit., p. 25.

11. Monique Gadant, *Islam et nationalisme en Algérie*, Paris: l'Harmattan, 1988, p. 25.

12. Roger Garaudy, *Biographie du Xxème siècle: Le testament philosophique de Roger Garaudy*, Paris: Édition Tougui, 1985, p. 288.

13. Details of French officers' dishonesty are found in Lucile Provost, *La deuxième guerre d'Algérie*, Paris: Flammarion, 1996, p. 10, and Michel Chodkiewicz, *Emir Abd el-Kader: Ecrits spirituels*, Paris: Seuil, 1982, pp. 16 & 19.

14. Roger Garaudy, *Pour un dialogue des civilisations*, op. cit., pp. 56-65.

15. Government Inquiry Commision Report 1883, quoted in ibid., p. 60.

16. Ibid., pp. 62-63.

17. Ibid., p. 65.

18. Cited in Mahsas, op. cit., p. 337.

19. Ibid.

20. Ibid., p. 333.

21. Monique Gadant, op. cit., p. 25. The term 'Church' in the quotation was put between quotes by myself.

22. Idem.

23. Benyoucef Ben Khedda, *Les origines du 1er novembre 1954*, Algiers: Éditions Dahlab, 1989, p. 70.

24. Ahmed Mahsas, op. cit., p. 336.

25. Alfred Grosser, *Affaires extérieures: la politique de la France 1944-1984*, Paris, Flammarion, 1984, p. 149.

26. Mohamed Harbi, *L'Algérie et son destin: Croyants ou Citoyens?*, Paris, Arcantère Éditions, p. 66.

27. ENA was accused of 'separatism' by France and of preventing Muslims from responding to the PCF's appeal to join in the fight against Franco's fascist Spain. See Benyoucef Ben Khedda, *Les origines du 1er Novembre 1954*, op. cit., p. 73.

28. Idem, p. 55, footnote 1.

29. Idem, pp. 109-111. Also, Ahmed Mahsas, op. cit., pp. 204-207.

30. Khedda, op. cit., Annex 3, p. 262.

31. Malek Bennabi, *The Problem of Ideas in the Muslim World*, co-published by Budaya Ilmu, Sdn. Bhd. And Dar al Hadara (Cal.), 1994, pp. 76 & 78.

32. Mahsas, op. cit., p. 132. This was expressed by Shaykh Ben Bādīs in a famous ideological poem which says, in substance: 'The Algerian people is Muslim and to Arabism it belongs, whoever says it has parted with its origin or says it is dead is indeed a liar, or [whoever] accuses it of integration, is saying the impossible.'

33. Roger Garaudy, *Biographie du XXème Siècle: Le testament philosophique de Roger Garaudy*, Paris Editions Tougui, 1985, p. 288.

34. Ibid., p. 292.

35. Ibid. For her part, Monique Gadant, op. cit., p. 24, argues that the policy of the ʿulamāʾ was 'a questioning of all the cultural policy of France'. See also Benyoucef Ben Khedda, op. cit. and Ahmed Mahsas, op. cit.

36. Lucile Provost, op. cit. p. 11.

37. According to Emir Khaled (reported by Benyoucef Ben Khedda, op. cit., p.43), 80,000 Algerians were sacrificed also during World War I. Figures of the Algerians who died for France in Indochina are not available, but what is saddening is that France used Muslims to kill other Muslims in its 19th and 20th centuries wars: it used Algerians and Senegalese Muslim infantarymen to crush Abdelkarim el-Khattabi's resistance in the Moroccan Rif; it used Moroccans against the Algerian resistance; and used Algerians and Moroccans against Syrian Muslims.

38. Ferhat Abbas, *L'indépendance confisquée*, Paris: Flammarion,

1984, p. 46.

39. Monique Gadant, op. cit., p. 9.

40. Malek Bennabi, *The Problem of Ideas in the Muslim World*, trans. Mohamed T. Mesawi, Malaysia/California, copub. Budaya Ilmu Sdn. Bhd./Dar al Hadara, 1994, pp. 112-114.

41. Monique Gadant, op. cit., p. 19.

42. Idem. p. 31.

43. Malek Bennabi, op. cit., p. 112-113.

44. This view tallies with data obtained from an Algerian veteran of the war of liberation and prominent official in independent Algeria, who told us that 5,000 Algerians, instructed by French experts in neighbouring Morocco, were repatriated at the time of independence for the purpose of taking over the new Algerian state's administration and government machinery from the French. Many of them, with French nationality and/or wives, have reached the higher spheres of power without disclosing their French connection (See Lucile Provost, *La deuxième guerre d'Algérie*, Paris, Flammarion, 1996, p. 33). They constitute France's fifth column, the strategic core of what is known as the *Hizb Fransa* or the 'party of France.'

45. Dr. Tawfīq al-Shāwī, *Safahāt min Daftar al-Dhikrayāt* (excerpts from the author's *Memoirs*), 44th part, in *Al-Mujtama'* no. 1146, 18th April 1995, p. 46. The statement is based on 'realities and documents' to be found in a book written by Fathi al-Dib, a former Egyptian security services officer under Nasser's rule, who was at the same time Vice Deputy Secretary General of the *Arab League* in 1954.

46. Shaykh al-Bashīr al-Ibrāhīmī, leader of the *'Ulamā' Association*, was the first to be put under house arrest immediately after independence, followed by other Muslim scholars and intellecuals who set up the *al-Qiyam* (Values) *Society* in 1964 to resist peacefully the 'official' imposition of Marxism in that year.

47. In fact, France's anti-Islamic approach applied to the whole Maghreb. It was inaugurated towards 1955 with the collaboration of Tunisia's former life President Bourguiba (who closed down *al-Zaituna*, the flagship of Islamic learning and culture in the Maghreb, as soon as he came to power in 1956). It was also facilitated by the

connivance of Nasser's Egyptian security services, according to Dr. Tawfīq al-Shāwī whose *Memoirs* (see previous footnote) are among the extremely rare accounts that give the Islamic point of view on this episode of the Maghreb and are very revealing in this respect.

48. It might be argued that since Algeria is the richest country of the Maghreb, its escaping from French influence is likely to turn the whole Maghreb into a group of Islamic states, especially given the strong Islamic revival in the whole region.

49. *La deuxième guerre d'Algérie*, op. cit., p. 20.

50. In his writings, Seyyed Quṭb remembered one of the Algerian *ʿulamā'* asking him in 1965 in Egypt to help the Algerian *ʿulamā'* table an Islamic constitution to stave off the new Marxist onslaught in Algeria. The Egyptian *ʿālim* referred him to his books.

51. See among others, Bouhout el Mellouki Riffi, *La politique française de coopération avec les Etats du Maghreb*, Paris: Publisud, 1989, pp. 90-94.

52. Whatever its importance, French aid was generally granted under the condition that contracts favoured French businesses. See Lucile Provost, op. cit.

53. Ibid., p. 104.

54. Quoted in *Le drame algérien: des gouvernments français complices*, [The Algerian Tragedy: the Complicity of French governments], *L'esprit libre*, May 1996.

55. Lucile Provost, op. cit., p. 40.

56. See *L'esprit Libre*, op. cit., as well as Lucile Provost, op. cit., pp. 37 and 40.

57. For these two quotations see Lucile Provost, op. cit., p. 33.

58. *L'esprit Libre*, op. cit.

59. See Lucile Provost, op. cit., pp. 36-37.

60. Abdelhamid Brahimi, *L'Algérie actuelle: crises et mutations en gestation*, lecture given at the School of Oriental and African Studies (SOAS) under the aegis of the Geopolitics and International Boundaries Research Centre and the Society for Algerian Studies, 2nd June, 1994.

61. *L'esprit libre*, op. cit., p. 29

62. Provost, op. cit., p. 41.

63. See Saad Dahlab, *Mission Accomplie*, Editions Dahlab, 1990, Annexe 10, p. 334.

64. From 1963 to 1969 Algeria received 22% of France's Foreign Ministry's cultural cooperation budget (see, *Politique étrangère*, vol. 58 (4) winter 1993-94). In the 1990s, much the same budget has been devoted to Algeria (see Lucile Provost, op. cit.). This underlines, if need be, the importance France gives to the cultural factor in its hegemonic strategy.

65. In fact the French daily *Le Monde* revealed in the mid-eighties the existence of over 36 French primary schools, the intake of which included 80% of children from the ruling class. Four French lycées existed until the 1980s when three of them were closed down.

66. The late ideologue Malek Bennabi, in his secret lectures in Algiers, used to argue that the ordinary man in Algeria would take a decade or so to notice this 'invisible' French cultural invasion simply because the French were no longer present physically as a colonial power.

67. After being briefly given the post of Director of Higher Education under Ben Bella (in the mid-1960s), he was allowed to contribute a few articles to the ruling FLN party weekly *Revolution Africaine*, before being pushed into anonymity. He nevertheless continued by training students secretly in Islamic political thought at his home until 1972 when the Algeria security got wind of the meetings.

68. For example, Shaykh Abdel Latif Soltani, *Al-Mazdakīya hiya aṣl al-Ishtirākīya*; Shaykh Mohamed al-'Arbawi, *al-Iʿtiṣām bi'l-Islām*.

69. For this, see Ali Waliken, 'Language and Personality', in *The Message International* (USA), January 1993.

70. Lucile Provost, op. cit., pp. 66, 67 and 102.

71. Arabophone Prime Minister Mohamed M'Zali of Tunisia (1980-1984) had a similar experience: he was sacked, following French pressure on President Bourguiba, three months after his decision to arabize the first four years of primary education in 1984.

72. Ali Waliken, *Language and Personality*, op. cit.

73. *Le Monde*, 1st July 1992. Ironically, at about the same time, Jean d'Ormesson, a prominent French figure, was defending on television the French language which was threatened by the growing invasion of English words, explaining to the public how the French language reflected French people's personality.

74. The following data were obtained from Algerian senior academic staff who cannot be named in view of the consequences which they will suffer if they are identified.

75. Idem.

76. Lucile Provost, op. cit., pp. 20-21.

77. *The Washington Report*, April-May 1995, p. 20.

78. The French daily *Libération*, Editorial, p. 7, 24th October 1995.

79. The number of casualties was consistently belittled in the French press which reported 'over 600'. One doctor in the central hospital privately revealed at that time that 1,500 youths had limbs amputated in the five days of the uprising, due to the use of explosive bullets by the army.

80. Lucile Provost, op. cit., p. 101.

81. Abdelhamid Brahimi, *L'Algérie actuelle: crises et mutations en gestation*, op. cit.

82. *The Washington Report*, op. cit.

83. The French daily, *Canard Enchaîné*, 20th June 1990.

84. *L'Algérie en murmure: Un cahier sur la torture en Algérie*, Plan-Les-Ouates (Switzerland): Hoggar, 1996, p. 121, note 31.

85. Idem.

86. See, for example, *L'esprit Libre*, op. cit.

87. Moussa Aït-Embarek, *L'Algérie en murmure*, op. cit., p. 127 confirms this and gives ample details on the consultations between the Algerian generals, their French counterparts, and the Élysée over the possible ways to stop FIS from coming to power.

88. Lucile Provost, op. cit., p. 84. See also Moussa Aït-Embarek, *L'Algérie en murmure*, op. cit., p. 121.

89. See *Le Monde*, 8th July 1995.

90. Ibid., 24th January, 1995.

91. For a thorough and cogent account of the French media

manipulation of the Algerian situation after 1988, see François Burgat, *L'Islamisme en face*, Paris: La découverte, 1995, pp. 155-175.

92. A prominent FIS leader after the imprisonment of the party's founders and leaders Abbassi Madani and Ali Belhadj. He was assassinated, along with at least forty-five other intellectuals, by Algerian security agents who had infiltrated into the *Armed Islamic Group* (GIA) in November 1995.

93. See, among others, François Burgat, *L'Islamisme en face*, op. cit. p. 170.

94. For revealing details on individual atrocities committed against intellectuals, children, women, and French people, and widely blamed on the Islamic movement, see ibid., pp. 172-175.

95. Ibid., p. 163.

96. In 1995, the BBC World Service ran a series of programmes entitled *The Legacy of Colonialism*. The interviews in the countries mentioned here showed the way ordinary people felt about the present French domination of their respective countries culturally and economically. The BBC could not produce a similar programme on Algeria due to the situation there.

97. In a lecture on 24th June 1996 (the British Parliament, Grand Committee Room) organized by the international NGO *Just World*, the R. H. Jeremy Corbin MP described cogently the mechanisms and tools used nowadays by the North to submit the South economically to a new form of imperialist manipulation.

98. Jacques Lafont, 'La bombe et la culture', in *Le Monde*, 29-30 October 1995.

99. Jean-Franois Daguzan, 'Les rapports franco-algériens, 1962-1992: Réconciliation ou conciliation permanente?', in *Politique étrangère*, vol.58 (4), Winter 1993-1994.

100. *La deuxième guerre d'Algérie*, op. cit., p. 23.

101. When the various secular and Islamic opposition parties reached a common agreement, known as the Rome Platform, under the aegis of the Sant' Egidio Christian order (Rome, January 1995), Paris merely made some vague, non-committal statements, while individually some officials mocked it. The presence of the Islamic

Front among the signatories of the agreement was not welcome.

102. Algerian Islamists' estimates based on figures supplied by the *Independent Algerian Committee for the Defence of Human Dignity and Human Rights* put the toll at about 120,000 people killed, mostly young people, between 1992 and 1996. *Le Monde*, usually very 'conservative', acknowledges the 'unofficial' figure of 80,000 at the end of last spring.

103. Edward Said, *Culture and Imperialism*, London: Vintage, 1994, p. 17.

104. *France-Inter* radio station programme on French cinema, 4/10/1996.

105. Courageous indeed have been the voices of such intellectually upright and farsighted writers and thinkers like Roger Garaudy, Francois Burgat, and Pierre Guillard to mention but these, some of whom who have received anonymous threats to their lives.

CHAPTER II

ALGERIAN SUFISM IN THE COLONIAL PERIOD

Omar Benaissa

This chapter will explore some of the principal themes of Sufism in the colonial period, both from the point of view of the colonized and the colonizers. The most important point that needs to be stressed at the outset is that, however much the Sufis have been characterized as superstitious 'marabouts' – by both orientalists and modernizing Muslims alike – it was largely thanks to the influence of Sufism that a basic piety and spirituality were sustained throughout the colonial period. Furthermore, if it be remembered that colonialism was, essentially, an assault on the traditional Islamic way of life and accompanying modes of thought, then one can conceive of no strategy of 'resistance' more effective and fundamental than that pursued by the Sufis. Paradoxically, it was those whose concern was in essence 'otherworldly' that proved the most successful in concretely thwarting the colonial designs of the French, thus proving the efficacy that flows from the practice of the Sufi ideal: 'Be in the world, but not *of* it.'

Before addressing these themes directly, it may be helpful to provide a briefly sketched back-ground describing the overall institutional forms taken by Sufism at this time; and this means, essentially, giving a brief overview of the major Sufi orders and their leading shaykhs in Algeria under colonialism.

In the first third of the nineteenth century, when France embarked upon the colonial conquest of North Africa, Sufism was already organized in the form of religious orders. In their book entitled *Les confréries religieuses musulmanes*, Depont and Coppolani numbered twenty three of them throughout the country in 1897.[1] Some of them originated from the East (Syria, Iran, Turkey) and settled in North Africa as local branches, still connected to their eastern headquarters. Others became independent, no longer beholden to the shaykhs of the East; they were even named after their local founder or renovator.

One of the most prominent of these latter was the *Tijānīyya* order which was founded by shaykh Abu-l-ʿAbbās Aḥmad b. Muḥammad b. al-Mukhtār b. Sālim al-Tijānī who was born in 1738 in Ain Mādhi, some 72 km east of Laghouāt (Algeria) and died in Fez in 1815, i.e. fifteen years before the conquest of Algeria by France. Shaykh Aḥmad al-Tijānī was one of the greatest masters of Sufism that the Algerian land has ever given birth to during the last centuries. His teaching can be found in the *Jawāhir al-maʿānī*, compiled by his disciple ʿAli b. Harāzim. Shaykh Aḥmad al-Tijānī was an exceptional figure who still commands respect and attention within Sufi circles as well as among the general seekers after the inner truths of religion. Before creating his own order which was destined to spread throughout Saharan Africa, he had been an affiliate of the *Khalwatīyya*, founded in Iran by Muhammad al-Khalwatī al-Khawārizmī (who died in 751/1350). His order was based in Ain Mādhi, near Laghouat. But, after the attack of the Turks who feared the emergence of a rival power, he took refuge in Morocco in 1799, where he was warmly welcomed by Sultan Mulay Sliman. After his death, his successors returned to Ain Mādhi and spread further the presence and influence of the order.

His second son, and also his successor, refused to give allegiance to Emir Abdelkader. The latter besieged the fort of Ain Mādhi for six full months, from June to the end of November 1838. Abdelkader, surprised by the resistance of the besieged, was compelled to come to an agreement which allowed the Tijānī leader to leave the town, without recognising the Emir's authority. After the French victory, the *Tijānīyya* was re-established in Ain Mādhi, and gradually gained the confidence of the new masters of the country.

The *Tijānīyya* offers the most eloquent example of the orders' dynamism, even under the hard conditions of colonialism; it proved its spiritual efficacy in various ways, but particularly through its propagation of Islam in the African lands coveted by Christian missionaries. No less than thirty million Africans took up Islam, thanks to this order, according to Miftāḥ ʿAbd al-Bāqī.[2] Even if the figure seems somewhat exaggerated, it does indicate that the colonial authorities were unable to inhibit the activity of this order. With the approach of independence in 1954, the *Tijānīyya* suffered an overall decline; and today, in numerical terms, it is the third largest order in the country and the largest in the Saharan regions.

Just before the *Tijānīyya*, another important order had been founded; this was the *Raḥmānīyya*, which also stemmed from the *Khalwatīyya*, and which was to play a prominent role during the Kabyle resistance to the colonial onslaught. The *Raḥmānīyya* was founded by Muḥammad b. ʿAbd al-Raḥmān al-Jarjarāʾī (who died in 1793-94), also named Bou Qabrayn, i.e. the double-tombed man. Today, Sīdi Muhammad is still the second patron saint of the Algerian capital, known as *Moul lebled*. Captain De Neveu wrote in 1845: 'Ben Abd er-Rahman's order is really the National Order of Algeria. It has been given birth within Algeria; it has been founded by a native of Algiers. Who knows if this reason has not determined Mahi-ed-Dīn's son (Emir Abdelkader) to prefer it to any other.'[3]

In 1897, it was the most widespread order with 177 *zāwiyas*, 140,596 male adepts and 13,186 female adepts; and these figures are certainly below the true number, according to Depont and Coppolani. The *Raḥmānīyya* is not only regarded by many as the Algerian order *par excellence*, it is also seen as the 'National Church of Kabylia', to use Mouloud Mammeri's expression, who also notes that 'since independence, this order has undergone a real revival of activity.'[4]

In a short article published in 1961, one year before the independence of Algeria, the review *l'Afrique et l'Asie* wrote in its 55th issue: 'Towards 1950, the orders as a whole numbered some 500,000 adepts divided into four main orders: the *Qādirīyya*, the *Khalwatīya*, the

Shādhilīyya and the *Khādhirīyya*. Numerically, the *Rahmānīyya*, connected to the *Khalwatīyya*, comes first with nearly 230,000 adepts, most of them Berbers.'

It is during the first decade of the French occupation (1830-1840) that the famous saint, shaykh Mohand ul-Hosin was born in Kabylia which was then still free. He died at the beginning of the present century and had belonged to this order before retiring.

In 1823, the *Darqāwa* was founded by Sidi al-ʿArabī al-Darqāwī in Morocco, but this *ṭarīqa*, stemming from the *Shādhilīyya*, had an important ramification, especially in western Algeria. In 1845, De Neveu spoke about it in these words: 'They are dangerous fanatics, always ready to seize any opportunity to raise peaceful peoples against the authorities. As a matter of fact, the *Darqāwa* is no more a religious sect, it has turned into a political faction that has constantly been hostile to the Turks.'5

After the French occupation, another local order, which will have a major influence in Libya, was given birth in the region of Mostaganem. It is the *Sanūsīyya*, founded in 1253/1837 by Sayyid Muḥammad ibn ʿAli al-Sanūsī (who was born in 1202/1783 and died in 1276/1859).

Another major order, perhaps the oldest to be established in the country, and the one which was to manifest fierce resistance to the French invasion was the *Qādirīyya*, which spread, in western Algeria, mainly in Oran and its surroundings, and to which belonged the famous Emir Abdelkader (ʿAbd al-Qādir al-Jazāʾirī). The *Qādirīyya* and the *Khalwatīyya* spread in Turkey, too, where they had many adepts, among the political and social elite as well as the ordinary folk.

To complete this brief table of the situation of Sufism, one must include some smaller orders, stemming from the *Darqāwīyya*, such as the *Hebrīyya*, also called *BuʿAzzāwīyya*, born in Morocco, but with a ramification in Algeria, and the *ʿAlawīyya*, well after the 'pacification' of the country by the French, in the beginning of the 20th century. The *Hebrīyya ṭarīqa*, which Depont and Coppolani ignored, developed mainly in the north-west of Algeria and numbered 6,000 followers in

1953, according to General André.[6] Such, then, were the major orders in Algeria; and, as can be seen from the number of their adherents alone, their influence on Algerian society could not be ignored.

The colonial elites rapidly addressed themselves to the task of investigating the orders, both in respect of their teaching and their organization. It was an urgent necessity for the effective management of the conquered territories. Exhaustive catalogues were progressively drawn up by colonial officers, anxious to collect information to be used immediately. Later on, the collected information was used by orientalists, some of whom, albeit working in France's colonial interests, also attempted to carry out scientific work and scholarly research.

The first orientalists were officers in charge of collecting information likely to be useful for the generals' strategies; this they did on site, not from books. One might refer here to Captain De Neveu's book entitled *Les Khouans, ordres religieux chez les musulmans de l'Algérie*, published in Paris in 1845 (Abdelkader's resistance came to an end in 1847), the content of which consists of oral information collected directly from the adepts of the different religious orders under scrutiny.[7]

However, our focus here is not so much on the military and political aspects of the encounter between Sufism and colonialism, but on the light which a careful reading of the colonial authors' and the orientalists' work can shed on the underlying spiritual and cultural dynamics of this encounter.

Sufism during the colonial period can be approached from different angles: organization, legitimacy, teaching, doctrine, and so on. Our study of Sufism during the colonial period will be an attempt to elucidate, through concrete examples, the relations that were established both objectively and subjectively between the two parties, the Sufis and the Europeans.

We shall focus here on two aspects of Algerian Sufism during the one and a half centuries of French colonization: first, Sufism as discovered and gradually studied by the occupiers, then Sufism such as it was capable of maintaining itself and surviving within a society which had materially lost everything, including even the semblance of its formal independence and liberty.

THE ORIENTALISTS

The study of Sufism and the religious orders by the orientalists is not merely descriptive. Certainly, there was a need to attend to the most urgent things, to meet the requirements of the new administration which sought to know the adversary. But some authors do not hesitate to propose theoretical explanations, to put forward hypotheses, founded on poor information obtained at the outset. They sought the reasons for the development of Sufism, or even the laws which govern it. They wondered about its educational efficacy, its strength, its organization, and its energy. And, it must be said, the result of their work is considerable. Some works still remain primary sources, both from the point of view of information and methodology. We are especially thinking of the works of L. Rinn, O. Depont and X. Coppolani, and E. Doutté, in France, of Goldziher in German orientalism and of many others.

In a famous article, headed *Le culte des saints chez les musulmans* published in 1880 in *La Revue de l'Histoire des Religions,* Goldziher laid down, for the first time, the 'scientific' foundations of the study of sanctity in Islam. Many of his observations deserve the careful attention of researchers. It must be said that Goldziher is not at all concerned about the 'civilizing mission' so dear to the French. His research is not determined by administrative constraints.

This considerable work achieved by men with the double purpose of serving colonization and science, can be considered, now, as a literature showing the French the way to the gradual discovery of Islam. A textual analysis may give us evidence that this struggle of the French against Islam was in fact a struggle of the French against themselves, against a certain state of mind, in order to overcome their own complex towards Islam.

So, the question will be asked, what did the French think of Sufism? We will base our answer on three examples, corresponding to three types of reaction: the reaction of the European in favour of colonialism, that of the scientist, and that of the common citizen meeting Muslims and represented here by a doctor.

In their endeavour to understand Sufism, the orientalists are often contradictory. When they deal with religious orders, they cannot help emphasising their hostility to France and depict them as fanatic forces opposed to progress. They even blame the orders for not being in accordance with Islamic orthodoxy. The Prophet, it was argued, had never wanted intermediaries to stand between believers and God; but the 'marabouts' seemed to constitute a surrogate priesthood, a clergy who have no place within a Muslim society. Like a parasitic priesthood, they also imposed taxes on peasants who were already heavily taxed by the French.

In other words, the French employed a series of arguments used by 'orthodox' adversaries of Sufism from within Islam itself. But the French also employed a different argument, assuming the legitimacy of intercession: for one sees the colonialists contending with the Sufi shaykhs about the right to be intermediaries between believers and God, and implying that this role falls to them.

In an article entitled *Les confréries musulmanes nord-africaines* published in 1923, P. Bruzon argues first, that 'the Prophet of Islam had a genius for preserving his doctrine from the evils which were ravaging Christianity and Judaism', that is to say, the clergy's pride and the doctors' arrogance and vanity. He drew the conclusion that 'maraboutism' is condemned by Islam. Then, he demonstrates that this phenomenon and its superstitions have originated from the Berber genius which, like the Persian genius, was anthropomorphist and could not sustain itself without guides and miracles. The Arab conqueror's mind allowed itself, unwittingly, to be 'contaminated' by the mind of the peoples it had conquered. We find here the kind of racial explanation that characterized social and anthropological theories of the 19th century.

After listing the orders, Bruzon proffers some recommendations as to how to behave towards the *sherifs* (that is, the descendants of the Prophet, also known as *sayyids*) and the marabouts: 'Whether he is a sherif or a marabout, the man who aims at playing any religious role to the prejudice of Muslim orthodoxy, should always arouse suspicion. There is every chance that such a man is just an ambitious one … We must not let him believe that he is the essential servant for our policy. We would be wise to receive his most vehement protestations of friendship with some scepticism … By definition, a religious order, a sect, is far too exclusive a social element to be relied upon. Its purpose must inevitably differ from ours. Why should it yield to us? … Whenever one of their leaders is in favour of us, we must be convinced that this is because he sees it as serving his own interests to be so.'

However, the author notes, 'Fortunately there exists another strong lever which can help us set the North African Muslim world on the way to a better destiny. This lever is, simply, orthodoxy.' Thereupon he mentions the name of Muḥammad ʿAbduh who 'admits the principles of evolution and proclaims the necessity of progress'. This last remark and those before it show clearly that the ʿālim is perceived by this author as being better disposed towards France than the *shaykh*.

Another – more intelligent – attitude is evinced in an article of Augustin Berque, the father of J. Berque – another famous French orientalist who died in 1995. He writes: 'The invasion of maraboutism, since the French conquest, and particularly between 1860 and 1900, can be explained by the diminution of the opposing forces which had contained it before … [those forces] whose decline has been hastened by the higher purpose of our civilizing action …' The influence of the *zaouia*, he continues, has suddenly increased for it has an open field: 'It remains the only attractive centre in the Arab country. And this results in a new polarization of influences which, for centuries, had been neutralising each other in the direction of the indigenous masses.'[8]

Now while it is no doubt true that the exoteric ʿ*ulamāʾ* have often inveighed against some of the excesses committed by Sufis, this should not be exaggerated and presented as all-out rivalry, or, still less, a permanent underlying conflict. But Berque and others like him did not want to admit that the more intensive mobilization of Sufi orders was simply the expression of a community's will to eject the colonialist. He preferred to look for another cause, in longer-term historical trends. However, as regards the fact that French influence diminished greatly the institutional influence of the *ʿulamāʾ* to the benefit of the less formal influence of the Sufis, his remark remains basically true.

It is also true that, even during the colonization, the *ʿulamāʾ* continued to criticize the actions and practices of certain orders, and tried to eradicate the 'maraboutism' which was regarded as the main obstacle to modernization. Ataturk was considered as a great renovator of Islam, even though he had not only shut the doors of the *tekkes* (equivalent in Turkey to the Maghrebi *zāwīyas* and the Iranian *khāneqahs*) of the countless orders which had hived off in Anatolia, but he also deprived the *ʿulamāʾ* themselves of all their powers. The diminution of the exoteric authorities does not necessarily result from the increase of Sufi influence, just as the development of Sufism cannot simply be adduced as a consequence of the weakness of its alleged adversary. The fact that two phenomena take place simultaneously does not mean that one is the cause of the other.

Be this as it may, Berque's position does have the advantage of showing that it is wrong to affirm *a priori* that the religious orders are pacifist and can easily be reconciled with any governing political power. They had taken up arms against corrupt Ottoman governors, even though they were Muslims; certain shaykhs in fact ordered uprisings against the *Beys* (Turkish governors) who were blamed for not acting according to the *Sharīʿa*. And, in Algeria, shaykhs were put under house arrest, or exiled, as was the case with Shaykh Aḥmad al-Tijānī, despite the fact that he had requested his adepts to be patient and restrained. The Oran *Bey* had prevented the father of the future Emir Abdelkader to go on the pilgrimage. Such facts as these should have suggested to Berque that these religious orders would have all the more reason to rise up against the French who, after all, were not even Muslims.

The political powers always knew instinctively to what extent they could control the orders, and the latter knew too how to set a limit to their ambition. However, on both sides, there had often been an attempt to dominate, if not to eliminate the other.[9]

Nevertheless, even if Berque's observation is quite original, it remains only partially true, and needs to be complemented and deepened by the realization that, confronted by an antagonist as powerful as colonialism, Sufism represented the last energy, the ultimate resource, the most deeply rooted dimension of Muslim society; for, in any society, the form taken by its final recourse reveals most clearly the authentic soul of that society. Algerian society defended itself by progressively mobilizing its energies because 'men feel that to unusual challenges we must give original answers.'[10] Naturally, Berque, and those orientalists who believed in the 'civilizing mission' of France, could not have seen things so sympathetically.

The last example to illustrate the way Sufism was percieved by the French, comes from the testament of a certain doctor, Marcel Carret, who relates in his *Souvenirs* – some excerpts of which are published in the biography by Martin Lings[11] – his meeting with Shaykh Aḥmad al-ʿAlawī whom he visited while he was sick :

> The first thing that struck me was his likeness to the usual representations of Christ. His clothes, so nearly if not exactly the same as those which Jesus must have worn, the fine lawn head-cloth which framed his face, his whole attitude, everything conspired to reinforce the likeness. It occured to me that such must have been the appearance of Christ when he received his diciples at the time when he was staying with Martha and Mary.[12]

This was written by a man who was a civilian and a doctor, but it is as an echo of another European testimony to Muslim sanctity; testimony given through a profound observation by a military man, Marshal Bugeaud, the 'pacifier' of Algeria. He depicts Emir Abdelkader, whom he had just met for the first time, to the Prime Minister, Count Molé, as follows: 'He is pale and is fairly like what has often been portrayed about Jesus.' The famous Algerian 'rebel' was still under forty years of age when he surrendered and had not yet reached full spiritual maturity. Michel Chodkiewicz, who mentions the fact in his introduction to the *Ecrits spirituels*, adds: 'This strong feeling is not produced only by the physical appearance of the personage. Bugeaud recognizes in the Emir a greatness which is beyond the reach of his soldierly categories, and attempts to define it in a letter of January 1st, 1846: "He is a sort of prophet, the hope of all Muslim devotees".'[13]

Another famous Frenchman, the unfortunate Leon Roche who pretended to embrace Islam in order to gain proximity to the Emir, witnessed in 1838 a nocturnal prayer by the Emir and his experience of a *ḥāl*, a mystical state. He notes: 'As I was sometimes favoured with the honour of spending the night in Abdelkader's tent, I could see him praying and I was struck by his mystical enthusiasm, but that night, he showed me the most striking expression of faith. That is the way the great saints of Christianity must have said their prayers.'[14]

It is surprising to see that, separated by a century, French Christians could discern in two figures of Islam, the Emir Abdelkader and the Shaykh al-ʿAlawī – two representatives of their 'faithless' adversaries – features which they do not hesitate to compare to those of Christ, their most sacrosanct figure and one to whom nobody would dare to compare supposedly faithless men. Other Christians were struck by the 'Christic' qualities of Muslim saints. Asín Palacios did not hesitate to entitle his work about Ibn ʿArabī *El islam cristian-izado*, and Louis Massignon was rightly struck by the likeness of Ḥallāj to Christ both in his life and the manner of his death: for, like Christ, Ḥallāj died on the cross.

Turning our attention now to the question of what the shaykhs were in fact doing during the colonial period, we shall present for consideration two concrete examples. Because of the Turkish debacle, the Algerians had grave difficulties in organizing a united resistance against the new invader. The country was not at all prepared to assume its own destiny, too trusting as it was in the Ottoman power, but most of all, too attached to a post-almohadian vision of the world: everything was done and decided within the limits of a tribe or the local shaykh. Official Islam, that of the ʿulamāʾ and their formal struc-tures, was entirely dependent on the other capitals of Islam (Cairo,

Damascus, and Istanbul). It was through the Sufi orders that Islam was able to acquire its local colour and integrate the masses more effectively.

The role of organizing the resistance to the French fell, therefore, to the shaykhs. Almost all the great masters of the orders went to the East before or after the French occupation. They all had at least the feeling of belonging to a community that transcended parochial frontiers, frontiers that would presently be rigidified by the colonial powers. Indeed, the temptation to leave everything and go to the elusive *Shām* (Syria) presented itself to many, including the Shaykh al-ʿAlawī and Shaykh Mohand.

SHAYKH MOHAND UL-HOSIN

During the armed resistance to the colonial occupation, the role of the shaykhs was to save that which could still be saved; but after the definitive victory of France, their role was to act as if the French colonial 'fact' were to last for centuries. Such was the attitude of Shaykh Mohand. Former *murīd* of Shaykh Mohand-Ameziane Ahaddad, leader of the *Rahmānīyya ṭarīqa*, he gradually separated from him. Shaykh Ahaddad, in spite of his age (he was 80), took the decision of supporting the 1871 anti-French revolt, and put 100,000 of his adepts and followers at the disposal of the Kabyle al-Moqrani, who wanted to take advantage of the French defeat by Germany (Sedan), and make a bid for independence. The Kabyles lost and Shaykh Ahaddad was sentenced to five years' imprisonment. To the judge who pronounced the sentence he answered: 'You have sentenced me to five years, but God has sentenced me to five days.' One of his companions asked him: 'Since you knew that we were going to lose, why did you call for the mobilization?' The shaykh answered: 'I wanted to set a definite gap between our children and France, so that they would not mix with French children and become like them. If there was no blood feud between us, a time would come when we would be unable to distinguish between a Muslim and a Christian. I have planted the tree of bitterness, the laurel, (*ilīlī* in Berber), so keep watering it and don't let it dry up.'[15] The shaykh died in Constantine five days after he had been sentenced.

Shaykh Mohand left his adepts free to choose whether to take part or not in the revolt, adding that as far as he was concerned, he would not interfere. He was to spend most of his life in his village of Ait Ahmed in the region of Ain al-Hammām. When he first entered Sufism, he was an itinerant dervish, wandering about with a group of companions, like the Persian *qalandars* of the 13th and 14th century. The most important personage of this group was Shaykh Mohand Wa`Alī who employed him as a shepherd. Towards 1871, during the French-German war, Shaykh Mohand became an accomplished master in his own right, initiating his own disciples into the spiritual path. He was a typically cenobitic saint, devoting his time to farming, cattle-breeding, and masonry.

Shaykh Mohand had definitely set aside, both in his thoughts and in his actions, any idea of an uprising against France. When asked on the matter he answered: 'France will not leave this country unless it is unfair', that is to say in expiation of its own injustice. He knew all too painfully how much the Kabyles – actually the Muslims as a whole – were divided, he knew how much they were consumed by vice, imperfection, injustice, all of which he witnesses every day.[16] He was indeed a witness of a sick society, one which had lost its unity, and which was unable to act as a single man. Nevertheless he remained close to the people; caring for them, comforting them, and re-establishing concord among them. When requested for a mediation, to settle a dispute, he would do so, and gave material assistance whenever he could afford it. Tradition relates that he was able to perform charismata, extraordinary feats, such as rescuing a drifting ship in which one of his *murīds* had invoked him, intervening from great distances to preempt the attempted killing of another disciple. But these actions were not performed with the aim of simply amazing people. All of his charismata are full of the mountaineer's sense of usefulness; they are of an eminently social nature.

People came to see him to obtain his blessing, his *baraka*, or to ask his advice on a project, on their work, or on family problems. His role as an arbitrator was such that the French conciliation magistrate in

Michelet (Ain al-Hammām) would visit him and ask how it was that he managed to solve disputes that he, the magistrate, could not. Indeed the Kabyles preferred the quick justice dispensed by a saint to a long drawn-out affair, ruinous for the ordinary man and, above all, presided over by a non-Muslim. This French magistrate also sought the shaykh's *baraka*.

He had nothing different from other men, he once answered to one of his *murīds*, except that he conformed more seriously to the will of God. Dermenghem evokes the social dimension of Shaykh Mohand's personality in the following terms:

> The social role of these cults for the tribe and the fraction ... is obvious. There has been, indeed, much abuse but also great service rendered, such as preaching, instructing and settling quarrels. I have collected these Kabyle *isefra* (poems) which give an idea of the conception of a saint in this country. It is about a saint who died in 1901. He asks his *khouans* (brothers) about the *awliya* (saints) and his disciples answer in these verses:

> 'Where are the *awliya*? The *awliya* are on the mountains. They are keeping guard. They are watching over the country with their eyes, without treading its ground. As soon as they see an injustice, they try to repair it'. And Shaykh Mohand answers to emphasize the practical usefulness of marabouts as well as their mystical value.

> 'And I say: Where are the *awliya*? They are in their houses. They are busy with the greater holy war [against egoism]. They are ploughing, they are providing for the need of their families. Oh God the merciful! I ask your help! '[17]

The shaykh was a man of action and a contemplative, one who could not easily contain his mystical states, but who gave expression to them thanks to his gift for poetry, a poetry that fed, educated, and developed minds, a poetry easy to memorize, so much so that his verses are still recited to this day in Kabylia. It is in these verses that we can discover the Shaykh's metaphysical doctrine.

The Shaykh belonged to a tradition of sanctity quite different from that of the Shaykh al-ʿAlawī, who was a saint of the city, and whose approach to spirituality was fundamentally intellectual: he discussed *waḥdat al-wujūd* (unicity of existence), the esoteric meaning of the prayer and the *ḥajj* (pilgrimage), and other philosophical doctrines, as we shall see later. Shaykh Mohand did not, strictly speaking, teach any doctrine. Neither the questions posed to him by his adepts, nor the answers he gave, dealt with any abstract or doctrinal developments on the nature of the Divine Being or any esoteric interpretations. He taught by means of his actions, an example which served to re-orient the hearts and minds of those around him, causing them to turn towards God, make them repent, and calm their passions. Like all other true Sufis, he had an innate sense of the essential in religion. The letter of the law was only referred to when he felt that his interlocutor needed it; otherwise, he always preferred to give priority to faith over actions: *'ifghīr win itswahiden Rebbi win itsabaden*: he who practises *tawḥīd* (i.e. he who, in all his actions, is never heedless of God's unique reality), is better than he who worships, who offers up but an external mode of prayer.

Among the Shaykh's *murīds*, there were many women, indeed, almost as many women as men, one would think. The most famous was his sister, another saint, named Lalla Fadhma. They are still often invoked together by old persons in Kabylia.

As regards the presence of France, he did not seem to take it into consideration. For him, the colonial fact was destined to be, and was thus the expression of the will of God; it was assimilated as the logical consequence of the actions of the Algerian people themselves, actions which had earned them such a decline. The solution to the problem was simple: the Muslims themselves had to change, to improve, so that God might grant them a better fate. This same spiritual logic held true also for the French: if they act in all fairness, they would keep the country, otherwise God would drive them out. On the plane of interpersonal relations, the same view of causality was evident, as for example in the following story

A certain man who had been in prison came to see the Shaykh. 'Where do you come from?', the Shaykh asked him. 'From the prison where you put me.' The man explained that, having betrayed one of the Shaykh's *murīds*, he thought that it was the Shaykh himself who had wished him to be sent to prison. Thereupon, the Shaykh answered: 'It is you who put yourself in prison.'

The mountain people of Kabylia believe in this way of looking at things, and they even think that the *awliyā'* are in fact the real leaders of the country, the real, albeit hidden, hierarchy through which authority flows.

SHAYKH AḤMAD AL-ʿALAWĪ

While France was celebrating the hundredth anniversary of its presence in Algeria, the reformists, led by Ben Bādīs (who died in 1942) and the Association of Algerian ʿUlamā', contaminated by the false hopes raised both by Wahhabism and Kemalism, also attempted to fight 'maraboutism' which, according to them, was spreading superstitions and keeping the people steeped in ignorance; in thus opposing Sufism in the name of Muslim orthodoxy they were playing the very role formulated for them by the colonialists.

And yet the latter, through one of their most informed intellectuals, gives evidence that flatly contradicts the notion that Sufis are ignorant and their influence regressive. In an article written two years after the death of the Shaykh Aḥmad al-ʿAlawī (July 14th 1934), A. Berque wrote in *La Revue Africaine*:

The biography of shaykh Ben `Aliwa (Ahmed would Mostefa) can be summarized in a few words. It essentially consists of ideas. He teaches an upsetting doctrine which is for many people a modern Gospel. For, just as he has a mass of ignorant affiliated people, he also has highly cultured European followers. His propaganda, nourished with a singular eloquence, an extensive knowledge, is tireless and fruitful ... We have known shaykh ben `Aliwa from 1921 to 1934. We have seen him slowly grow old. His intellectual enquiringness seemed to become sharper each day, and to his last breath, he remained a lover of metaphysical investigation. There are few problems which he had not broached, scarcely any philosophies whose essence he had not extracted.

In fact, this great figure, as described in the biography by Martin Lings, is first and foremost that of a man seeking knowledge. In the first years of his search, he took a wrong turn. He was initiated into the *ʿIsawiyya*, an order that had by that time degenerated to such an extent that its practices were dominated by tricks such as knife-swallowing and snake-charming. When he met the Shaykh al-Būzīdī, who was affiliated to the *Darqāwiyya*, he was earnestly in search of an authentic spiritual master. After charming a snake in front of the shaykh, he was asked whether he could tame a larger one; he replied that the size made no difference. The Shaykh al-Būzīdī then said to him:

> I will show you one that is bigger than this and far more venomous, and if you can take hold of it you are a real sage ... I mean your soul ... Go and do with that little snake whatever you usually do with them, and never go back to such practices again.[18]

It might be thought that the Sufi masters, deep in their meditation, did not pay much attention to wordly life, and that they lacked any real commitment to it. Certainly the case of Shaykh Mohand already shows the contrary, but one can also wonder whether this attitude of apparent other-worldliness is not in fact deeply concerned with the fundamental problems of the world; for the leitmotif of their teaching, the mainspring of all their action, is the deep conviction that, whatever the temporal circumstances may be, the real problem in life always remains that of the soul. An action which is not guided by a consciousness fixed on the Transcendent will come to nothing, according to this perspective, and it is bound to fail.

Such a perspective evidently informed the teachings of the Shaykh al-ʿAlawī, who hardly ever refers, in his writings, to the fact that his country is under French occupation. Even when, in his autobiography, he speaks of applying for a travel permit he does not mention the authority to which he had applied. Just back from a journey to the East which took him to Istanbul, he had the feeling that 'my return was sufficient as fruit of my travels, even if I had gained nothing else; and truly I had no peace of soul until the day when I set foot on Algerian soil, and I praised God for the ways of my people and their remaining in the faith of their fathers and grandfathers and following in the footsteps of the pious.'[19] It is obvious that, in the eyes of the

Shaykh al-ʿAlawī, Kemalism was much more dangerous than colonialism. Shaykh Mohand very likely had the same attitude.

As for the reformist ʿulamāʾ, the Shaykh al-ʿAlawī did not hesitate to put pen to paper and give them the stinging answers that their baseless criticisms called for. The weekly paper *al-Shihāb*, organ of the reformists, mounted repeated attacks on Sufism. To one such attack the Shaykh wrote a reply which was published in *al-Balāgh al-Jazāʾirī*. This was a spirited defence of Sufism, formulated in terms of Islamic orthodoxy, which argued that Sufism, as the inner spiritual dimension of Islam, had always been respected in the Islamic tradition. He supported his argument with an anthology of quotations, mostly from renowned exoteric authorities.

> There is no religious authority or man of learning in Islam who has not a due respect for the path of the Folk [a term designating the Sufis], either through direct experience of it in spiritual realization, or else through firm belief in it, except those who suffer from chronic shortsightedness and remissness and lack of aspiration ... God says: 'Whoso striveth after Us, verily We shall lead them upon Our paths,' [Qurʾān, XXIX: 69] and indeed the true believer looks unceasingly for one who will take him to God, or at the very least he looks for the spiritual gifts which lie hidden within him, that is, for the primordial human nature which he has lost sight of and in virtue of which he is human.

The Shaykh did not claim that the Sufis of his day were entirely blameless, however, and accepted that there were abuses, and that there were so-called Sufis – 'only too many' – who deserved censure. But, he concludes, 'What offended us was your vilification of the way of the Folk altogether, and your speaking ill of its men without making any exceptions, and this is what prompted me to put before you these quotations from some of the highest religious authorities. At the very least they should impel you to consider your brothers the Sufis as members of the community of true believers, every individual of whom both we and you are bound to respect.'

The Shaykh's role was not restricted to a select elite, abstracted from society at large; rather, the spiritual message he proclaimed radiated throughout the land in a manner that is difficult to quantify. A spiritual re-orientation of even one person in any milieu has potentially far-reaching repercussions; but it is clear that the Shaykh touched the lives of thousands. One disciple of the Shaykh, after describing the kind of spiritual method that one would adopt under the Shaykh's guidance, makes the following important point: ' ... a complete break had been made between him [the disciple] and his former life. Some of them for example had been to all appearances just ordinary manual labourers for whom, apart from their work, life had meant no more than begetting children and sitting in cafés. But now their interests were all centred upon God, and their great joy was to perform the *dhikr* [the invocation of the Name of God].'[20]

Accounts of other disciples reveal that the Shaykh not only initiated thousands of people directly into the *tarīqa*, but also dispensed the 'oath of blessing', a secondary degree of initiation, to thousands more, as well as preaching to all those who gathered around him whenever he travelled in the country: 'You would find sitting in front of him hundreds, nay, thousands, with heads bowed as if birds were hovering around them and hearts full of awe and eyes wet with tears, in silent understanding of what they heard him say.'[21]

Through his *muqaddams* or representatives, also, his positive influence radiated throughout the country. One such representative wrote that he received into the *tarīqa* more than six thousand people, among whom many were in turn given permission to guide others. Another wrote that he was part of a group sent by the Shaykh to travel from tribe to tribe in the deserts, with instructions to accept nothing from the tribes other than that which was absolutely necessary. When asked about this, the *muqaddam* would reply: 'We have only come to you so that you may take guidance from us upon the path or at least that you may give us your oaths always to perform the prayers at the right time with as much piety as you can muster.'[22]

The encouragement to pray should be carefully noted here: it was not just the subtleties of metaphysics or the meaning of the greater holy war against the soul that these Sufis were imparting. They were concerned both with enhancing simple piety for the majority and with offering, to those that thirsted for it, the inner aspect of the religion. In thus following the letter of the exoteric Law while plumbing its esoteric spirit, they contributed to the maintenance of a pious ambience throughout society. This piety, it must be remembered, was the best form of defence against the more insidious, because less visible, forces of secularization that underlay the French *mission civilisatrice*; colonialism, as stressed at the outset, was not just an assault on external liberty, it was, much more, an attack on the traditional Muslim mentality and way of life. Judged in this light, no 'political' strategy aiming at independence could be more 'effective' and 'useful' than this fidelity to the spirit of Islam.

CONCLUSION

Simply to dismiss out of hand the role of Sufism in the colonial period is not tenable. Many modern Muslims view Sufis as having been either the lackeys of imperialism or the standard-bearers of the obscurantism to which Islam was reduced prior to the advent of colonialism. The two examples on which we have drawn show amply, however, that in the unfavourable circumstances of the time, Sufis played an important, perhaps indispensable, part in upholding the basic ethos of Islam in society as a whole; and that they did so in the service of what constitutes the spiritual quintessence of Islam. In playing this double role, they may be said to have offered the most effective resistance both to French colonialism as such and to the underlying cultural and psychological threat posed by French rule.

The elimination of the religious orders, wished by some ʿ*ulamā*ʾ and the colonial administration was not, then, the condition for the 'renaissance' of Algerian society. All the components of Muslim society showed passivity, inefficiency, and degeneration; but we can assert confidently that, among these components, the Sufi orders offered the strongest resistance to the triumphant military forces of colonialism and showed more vitality in combating, and more lucidity in understanding, its pernicious cultural influence. Just as the orders fought against the initial material onslaught of the French, so they were the most tenacious fighters against the cultural imperialism that came in the wake of the French victory; and in so doing the Sufis taught a key dimension of true independence, which is not just freedom from colonial rule but liberation from the false ideals of the secular, western worldview on which that rule was predicated. The message of Sufism can be summed up, then, in a few words: to be formally free but inwardly enslaved is far worse than being outwardly constrained but inwardly free; and true freedom lies in submission to the One that is the source of absolute freedom.∽

NOTES

1. Octave Depont and Xavier Coppolani, *Les confréries religieuses musulmanes*, Algiers, 1897.

2. In an unpublished manuscript, folio. 219.

3. Captain E. De Neveu – *Les Khouans, ordres religieux chez les musulmans de l'Algérie* – Paris, 1845, p. 64.

4. Mammeri, Mouloud, *Inna-yas Sheykh Mohand*, French and Kabyle introductions, notes and transcription of Shaykh Mohand's Kabyle sayings in Latin script, Algiers, 1990, p.35. French text.

5. De Neveu. op. cit., p.103.

6. General P.J. André – *Contribution à l'étude des confréries religieuses musulmanes* – Algiers: La Maison des Livres, 1956, p. 251.

7. See for example Ignace Goldziher, *Le culte des saints chez les musulmans*, in *Revue d'histoire des Religions*, Paris 1880; Edmond Doutté, *Magie et religion dans l'Afrique du Nord*, (Re-issue of the 1908 Algiers edition), Paris, 1984; P. Bruzon, *Les confréries musulmanes nord-africaines*, in *Orient et Occident*, vol. 2, 1923; A Berque, *Essai d'une bibliographie critique des confréries musulmanes algériennes*, in *Bulletin de la Société de Géographie d'Oran*, 1918; A. Berque, *Un mystique moderniste: le Cheikh Benalioua*, in *Revue Africaine*, N° 79, 1936.

8. A. Berque, *Essai d'une bibliographie critique*, op. cit., p. 164.

9. In fact, a cursory glance at the history of Islam shows that Sufism had already manifested resistance to non-Muslim invasion. In the 13th century Sufism organized an efficient resistance against the Mongols and managed to convert them and then to integrate them within Muslim society. Certainly they could not drive them out of the

classical frontiers of Islam, but the shaykhs who remained inside the domain conquered and governed by the Mongols, worked steadily to convert their conquerors, while in Syria an ʿālim as brilliant as Ibn Taymīyya denounced the false conversion of the Mongols and ordered Muslims to fight them tirelessly with the hope of creating a new Arab caliphate.

10. M. Mammeri, *Inna-yās*, op. cit., p. 36.

11. Martin Lings, – *A Sufi Saint of the Twentieth Century, Shaikh Aḥmad al-ʿAlawī. His spiritual heritage and legacy*, London: George Allen and Unwin, 1971, Ch.1.

12. Ibid., p. 14

13. Emir Abd el-Kader, *Ecrits spirituels* (excerpts from *Kitāb al-mawāqif*), presented and translated from the Arabic by Michel Chodkiewicz, Paris: Seuil, 1982.

14. Ibid., p. 18.

15. Mammeri, *Inna-yās*, op. cit., p. 50.

16. In this connection, it is interesting to note the predictions of Sufi shaykhs announcing to their people a calamity sent by God because of their own sins. Sometimes, this prediction is in the form of a saint's prayer asking God to punish men who no longer deserve the divine protection. Such was the case in Kabylia which, until 1857, had not been subjected to French colonization. The previous year, a local saint, Shaykh Ben ʿĪsā, witnessing the corruption that was gaining ground around him, invoked divine punishment upon the wicked: 'Oh God! The country is completely neglected, injustice grows in it, send it a tyrant of any nature!'

17. E. Dermenghem, *Le culte des saints dans l'Islam maghrébin* Paris: Gallimard, 1954, p. 18; and Mammeri, *Inna-yās*, op.cit .,pp. 75-7.

18. M. Lings, op. cit., p. 52.

19. Ibid., p. 78.

20. Ibid., p. 105.

21. Ibid., p. 102.

22. Ibid., p. 104.

CHAPTER III

THE ALGERIAN ISLAMIST MOVEMENT

Mohamed Gharib

Nowhere is the Islamist challenge more manifest than in Algeria. This was brought to the world's attention not only by the on-going armed Islamist insurgency but also by the consecutive electoral successes of the Islamic movement. The purpose of this paper is not merely to analyse this phenomenon historically, or tackle its different components, but also to understand why this movement is so strong in Algeria. The central focus of this paper is to show that this movement is a home-grown phenomenon that reflects deep social dynamics in Algeria. Hence, we believe that an exclusive reliance on political and economic analytic tools is not sufficient to understand a phenomenon that is primarily social and essentially cultural. It is a quest for identity and authenticity.

ALGERIAN 'ISLAMISM'

Islamism refers to the process whereby Islam is as it were 'ideologized' and reduced from the realm of spiritual belief to the domain of politics. Islam as a universal doctrine makes no rigid separation between the religious and the secular; but this universality has traditionally been determined by the spiritual principles of the faith in such a manner that the 'secular' is absorbed within the 'religious' sphere. Islamism, on the other hand, appears to secularize religion by applying its symbols and values to a programme very much determined by politically motivated goals. Islamism, then, refers also to the specific movements that use such an ideology as a reference point or a set of guidelines for their actions and as a 'ministry of mobilization' of the masses at a time when all the imported doctrines and ideological references have failed badly in post-independence Algeria.

The correlation between Islam and politics is not a new phenomenon in Algeria. In fact the respective resistance movements carried out against the French were done not only in the name of Algeria but of Islam. They were *jihāds* against infidel invaders. They were defined as compulsory acts, incumbent on all Muslims. The French further strengthened this conception of colonial relationships first by distinguishing Algerians from the settlers not by race, ethnicity or nationality but by religion for the Algerians, and geo-ethnicity for the settlers. Algerians were called 'Muslims' while the others were called 'Europeans'. This, and the consecutive French policies of selective assimilation that were aimed at stripping the Algerians of their Arabo-Islamic identity,[1] have not only further engrained this religious sense of identity but also strengthened the belief in the sole righteousness of the Islamic model. Islam was a source of identity and a motive for liberation. It was this identity that the Islamic reformist movement (The Association of Algerian *'Ulamā'*) was trying to establish and it was this motive that was later used by the FLN to mobilize the people around the nationalist agenda.[2]

In Algeria, Islamism is a home-grown phenomenon, despite the fact that it interacted with various foreign intellectual and religio-educational currents and was, consequently, influenced thereby. This influence goes as far back as World War I, when the youth that refused to join the French Army,[3] emigrated eastward and attended Tunisian and Middle-Eastern universities (Al-Zeitouna in Tunisia, Al-Azhar in Egypt and other religious institutions in the Levant and the Arab Peninsula).[4] These self-exiled students returned after the Great War influenced by the neo-reformism of Mohammad 'Abduh and Jamal al-Din al-Afghani. It was these students that established the Association of Algerian *'Ulamā'* that planted the first seeds of nationalism in Algeria.

The Islamic movement reflects not only the social and cultural fabric of society but also the very dynamics that shape change and which lead to either stability or instability. The development of this movement was additionally affected by the type of political culture and also the different cultural and intellectual currents flowing through society. Moreover, being a constituent part of the Muslim *Umma*, it is only natural that it would be affected by the intellectual and political debates that pass through this transnational entity. As far as Algeria is concerned, two factors helped predispose the country to these 'inter-Islamic influences': the lack of a strong scholarly tradition in Algeria; and the non-existence of highly qualified Islamic institutions (like al-Azhar or al-Zeitouna for example). There was therefore a vacuum that could only be filled by an external input.

One can de-construct foreign influence on Algerian Islamism into a three-level typology. The first category is intellectual in essence. In fact, several Algerian Islamists have been influenced by the thinking of the Muslim Brotherhood of Egypt and Syria, most notably Algerian students who studied in these two countries or those taught and influenced by Egyptian or Syrian teachers working in Algeria. An analysis of the theses elaborated by *Hamas* (led by Mahfoud Nahnah) and *Nahda* (led by Abdallah Djabballah) shows the depth of this influence,[5] not to mention the organic links that tie the former to the International Movement of the Muslim Brotherhood and the latter to the Tunisian *Nahda* movement presided over by the leading Islamist reformer, Rashed Ghannouchi.

The second type could be termed 'ideological influence'. A large portion of Algerian youth has been subjected to intensive Saudi (and *Salafi*) indoctrination. This Saudi policy was developed as part of its quest for the leadership of the Muslim world, and became extremely active in the aftermath of the oil booms of the 1970s that strengthened Saudi Arabia financially and reinforced its quest for leadership. It was the success of the Iranian Revolution, however, that made the Saudi state more determined to succeed in this undertaking by curtailing the Iranian (and *Shi'i*) challenge to its leadership, especially in view of the perceived success of the 'new Iran' in its premeditated confrontation with the United States (the hostage affair, the failure of the US military incursion into Iran), its severing of ties with Israel, and its manipulation of Islamic symbolism (e.g. the question of the liberation of Jerusalem). These successes induced the Saudi state to develop a new strategy focusing on two initial targets: discrediting the ideology of the Iranian Revolution (taken as an extreme form of Shī'ism) and re-capturing of the Islamic intellectual and 'ideological' arena.[6] To achieve these ends it developed a programme similar to that of the CPSU (Communist Party of the Soviet Union). This programme involved the distribution of free literature, the development of radio stations that could spread this message effectively in view of the high level of illiteracy in the Muslim world, giving grants to students from the Muslim world to come and take courses in Islamic studies in Saudi Arabia, etc. This strategy focused on the concept of *lā madhhabiyya* (no need to subscribe to the existing four Sunni schools of thought: Mālikī, Shāfi'ī, Ḥanbalī and Ḥanafī) as prescribed by Wahhabism or the Saudi state ideology. Through this approach, and with generous donations (private and public), the Saudi state managed to expand its influence on the evolution of Islamic political thought and movements. Of the countries in North Africa, Algeria has been the most affected by this type of influence, in view of the type of discourse propounded by certain known Salafis, like Ali Belhadj and others who focus on a narrow and literal reading of the scripture and who have constantly launched crusades against Shī'ism, Sufism, Western culture and political thought and who appear, to say the least, to be frustrated by the prospect of political modernity.

The final category could be termed 'methodic influence'. More than a thousand Algerians have served in the Afghan war[7] and returned indoctrinated with the thinking that refuses anything but their own concept of the caliphate according to the Islamic system of governance. They perceived the existing regime to be a legitimate target for their narrow conception of *jihād* (Holy War, or holy terror in their case). These Afghan veterans constitute the hardcore of the GIA (*Groupe Islamique Armé*), that subscribes to a radical internationalist movement. A careful reading of the program of the GIA[8] and a comparison between it and the book[9] written by the leader of the International Jihadi Movement (the Syrian Omar Abdelhakim, or Abu Mussabb) shows that the two movements and programs are similar in all important respects.

TYPOLOGY OF THE ALGERIAN ISLAMIC MOVEMENT

The Algerian Islamic movement, like all similar movements across the Muslim world, is neither homogeneous nor monolithic. In fact, it is composed of a plethora of groups, associations, and individuals with diverging programmes, strategies, policies, and political inclinations. This movement can be broken down into a three-level typology determined by the strategy of Islamization adopted by each category:

a) *Religio-political movements*: these are composed of Islamic welfare and religious groups, associations, and individuals that reject the state's monopoly on Islamic discourse and that strive to re-capture the initiative in this area from the authorities by promoting charitable, cultural, educational, and social activities. This is how all the politically-oriented Islamic Movements started in the 1960s and 1970s.[10] The associations, groups, and individuals comprising this category want to re-Islamize society through education, welfare, and the spread of the Islamic moral code. In the case of Algeria one can mention the examples of al-Qiyam ('Values') and Al-Irshād wa'l-Iṣlāḥ (the nucleus used by Nahnah to build his Islamist party, Hamas), and Al-Rābiṭa al-Islāmīyya ('The Islamic League') presided over by Shaykh Sahnoun and serving as an umbrella for all the currents of the Islamic Movement between 1988 and 1991 when the Islamic tendency was fragmented into three political parties (FIS, Hamas and Nahda); these parties were unwilling to cooperate with one another and often engaged in a number of polemics caused by personal differences.

b) *Politico-religious movements:* this category is composed of parties and organizations (FIS, Hamas, Nahda) which base their strategy on direct political participation in national politics through the political socialization and mobilization of the masses and by taking part in electoral contests. These parties and organizations generally subscribe to the goal of a non-violent transfer of power.

c) Radical Islamist movements: this last category is composed of a nebula of militant and hardline groups seeking the immediate trans-formation of both state and society through an insurgent strategy (the *Armed Islamic Movement* or MIA, the *Armed Islamic Group* or GIA, the *Islamic Salvation Army* or AIS).

This categorization is flexible, however, since several groups and/or individuals can roam from one category to the other depending on the degree of their political maturation and intellectual sophistication, internal political and socio-economic conditions, the level of state repression or the conditions under which political partic-ipation is permitted. It is evident that the more the regimes minimize political freedoms and basic rights of political participation, the more people perceive violence as the only way of introducing their ideals into the political arena.

Contrary to Western public and expert opinion, it is the Islamic politico-religious movement that constitutes the dominant 'opposi-tional discourse and activity' in Algeria.[11] This fact was blurred by the intense publicity given to the armed insurgency and particularly to the sensational actions of the GIA. The fact is that the majority of Algerian Islamists subscribe to 'the non-violent transfer of power and are moderate in political orientation' and that the radicals and militants are the exception and not the general rule.[12]

ISLAMIC RADICALISM AND THE ALGERIAN CONTEXT

Armed Islamist groups are not a novelty in post-colonial Algeria. The first example of armed insurgency was the one undertaken by the MIA (*Armed Islamic Movement*) from 1982 to 1987.[13] It was led by Bouyali Mustapha until his death on 3rd February 1987. Its activities were concentrated in Algiers and the surrounding department of Blida. Its most publicized action was the attack on the Police school in Soumaa in 1985 (30 kms to the South West of Algiers) in which one policeman was killed. The MIA constitutes the precursor of Islamic radicalism in Algeria.

The current armed groups in Algeria are not uniform ideologically, politically or institutionally. They are numerous despite the attempt of some leaders to unite them under one army as was the case with the *Congress for Unity May 1994* which brought together groups from different parts of the country. One can identify here the two most significant groups: GIA (*Armed Islamic Group*) and AIS (*Islamic Army for Salvation*) – the former because of its sensational actions that enabled it to grab the headlines, and the latter for its nationwide structure, its organization as an army, and its allegiance to the leadership of the FIS in prison (Abbassi Madani and Ali Belhadj).

AIS is the official military wing of the FIS. It is the best equipped armed Islamic group nowadays and is centrally controlled. It is presided over by Madani Mezrag. AIS was created in the spring of 1994 by the internal and clandestine leadership of the FIS when they realized that the movement was likely to be carried along by the GIA extremists in 'a fight to the death, [which] they wanted no part of'.[14] The AIS, which declared its allegiance to the leadership of the FIS in prison, tried to distance itself from the GIA by condemning the latter's terrorist acts, although it did not renounce armed conflict.[15] The AIS's main targets are the security forces. It is particularly responsible for attacks on the special forces (*Ninjas, Red Berets* and the commandos who constitute the hard-core of the anti-terrorist special forces). It has never claimed responsibility for the killings of civilians and foreigners and has always condemned such acts. According to the Paris-based *Observatoire des Pays Arabes* (OPA), the AIS has a membership of about 12000-15000 men.[16] This number is said to have increased since the publication of these statistics (November 1995) with the defection of a large section of the GIA after the assassination of Shaykh Mohamed Said, Abderrezak Redjam and over 140 other Islamists by fellow members of the GIA.

The GIA was created in 1993 as a result of the oppression orchestrated by the regime which radicalized the extreme fringes of the Islamist movement, which thereafter became disillusioned with any political discourse.[17] This constituted a serious strategic deviation by a cross-section of this movement from an essentially peaceful approach; it was a '… shift from the realm of politics to the field of terror'.[18] The first actions that put their name both in the anti-terrorist files and the media, was the assassination of foreigners (more than one hundred have been killed so far). They have also engaged in the most hideous and sickening operations by claiming responsibility for the killing of women, children, journalists, academics, lawyers, etc., and by raping women and mutilating bodies. This Group was composed, in 1995, of 2000-4000 armed insurgents (according to the OPA).[19] Nowadays, however, its strength is inferior to this because of the withdrawal of several sub-groups from it after the assassination (in November 1995) of 140 militants of the Djaz'arites[20] (or 'Algerianists', those subscribing to a typical Algerian model) that joined this group in May 1994. It was weakened further by the death of its leader (Djamal Zitouni) on 16 July 1996.[21] In fact, the GIA has now split into several factions, some of which have even engaged in a war of attrition against one other. It has split into two different doctrinal groupings: internationalist *Salafis* and parochial Algerianists. The three most important groups are: the GIA which is led by Zitouni's main aide, Antar Zouabri[22] (Abou Talha) and who is believed to be at least as radical as his predecessor. Another group subscribing to the same tendency (*Salafi*) is led by Hassan Abu Walid (Miloud Hebbi), commander of the Southern Zone (Laghouat, in the Sahara). The third group brought together several small units all subscribing to the Algerianist school of thought. This new group is called the *Front for Preaching and Jihad*, and is led by Mustapha Kertali, the former GIA 'emir' of Larbaa (20 km to the South of Algiers). This group comprises the most effective Algerianist armed group, FIDA, which was responsible for the killing of several top officials.

The organization of the GIA is unknown, but on the basis of several testimonies it is composed of several autonomous groups with no central control. The only link is the name, and nominal allegiance to the leadership.[23] Each group is free to carry out its own activities and there is no real accountability. This could be the reason why this group has been widely infiltrated by the anti-terrorist intelligence service, evidence of which is the killing of several top leaders of the GIA. In fact, according to a report by *Maghreb Confidentiel*[24] the authorities infiltrate this group by means of the following three tactics:

1) through false deserters who allegedly desert with their arms but only for intelligence purposes;

2) by using their (anti-terrorist intelligence) elements living in the inner cities which constitute the breeding ground for potential GIA members, and

3) by creating their own 'GIA' groups to carry out activities in the name of the GIA but in reality serving the strategy of the secret services. The authorities use such acts in their psychological warfare to convince public opinion that 'Islamism' is ruthless and indiscriminately kills children, women, intellectuals, Imams, and so on; and is destroying the educational, social, and economic structures of the state. Such psychological conditioning is not only meant to cut the Islamist insurgents from their popular base and turn the people against them, but also to legitimize the January 1992 *coup d'état*.

What is going on in Algeria at the moment has gone beyond the culture of protest that generally defines Islamist movements.[25] It is now at the stage of violent confrontation, all attempts at coexistence having failed. Such coexistence could have been possible had the military not intervened to suppress the main Islamist party (FIS), which won two successive elections, depriving them of the right to become the first democratically elected government in the Maghreb.

THE POLITICO-RELIGIOUS DIMENSION OF THE ALGERIAN ISLAMIC MOVEMENT

When Algeria recovered its independence in 1962, after 132 years of colonial subjugation and exploitation, politics was to be dominated by the FLN (*Front de Libération Nationale*), since all the pre-existing parties and political tendencies were forced to dissolve within the Front that was spearheading the anti-colonial revolution. The *Association of ʿUlamā'* was no exception since it was also integrated institutionally into the Front in 1956.

The FLN and the new 'army-party hierarchy'[26] held a monopoly not only on political activism but also on Islamic discourse, since this was an important requirement for the success of its strategy of political legitimation. It created a ministry of religious affairs to supervise, regulate, and administer religious activities. In order to ensure ideological compliance, it transformed Islamic scholars and preachers into civil servants of the state and deterred any Islamic activity outside this 'official framework'. It inherited and exploited to the limit the 'Badissian' (after Ibn Bādīs, the founder of the *Association of Algerian 'Ulamā'*) trilogy ('Islam is my religion, Arabic is my language and Algeria is my country') and all the symbolism attached to it. This was part of the strategy of political legitimation.

This 'State Islam' was, however, confronted by three challenges from the very start: the first was from within the army-party hierarchy, that is, from former militants of the *Association of 'Ulamā'* who remained either within the FLN or within the Army after taking its new name, *Armée Nationale Populaire* (ANP). These militants preferred to remain within these formalized frameworks either for personal reasons, or for fear of bifurcating the political scene by working outside this framework when Algeria was in need of stability and unity; also because of a conviction in the possibility of actively contributing to the application of the November 1954 Declaration that endorsed the reformist ideals of the *'ulamā'*. These people opposed the socialist policies of the left, and the state was forced not only to moderate the socialist-inspired programmes of reform but also to dig deep into Islamic thought to legitimize these new ideological and programmatic choices. It thus equated socialism with the Islamic concept of social equity and innovated in political terminology, trying to reconcile these two distinct paradigms and sets of principles. 'Islamic Socialism' was the outcome of this ideological sophistry.

The second challenge came from organized associations. The precursor of such undertakings was the formation of the association of 'Values' (*al-Qiyam*). This association was established in 1963 and obtained legal accreditation on 14th February 1963. It was presided by El Hachemi Tidjani.[27] This association was active in opposing the ideological choices of the regime and in upgrading the respect for

Islamic values and ethics in the construction of the new Algeria. This association was elitist in its composition and intellectual in its rhetoric. It tried to propagate its Islamic vision by holding conferences and lectures and by publishing a journal called *al-Tahdhīb al-Islāmī* ('Review of Muslim Education'). It focused in its discourse on the neo-reformist ideas of the *Association of Algerian 'Ulamā'* and even the more radical theses of Sayyid Qutb, along with some of the ideas contained in the doctrine of the Egyptian Muslim Brotherhood.

Despite a few incursions into the realm of politics, this association was focusing the whole of its work on social, educational, and moral issues. However, because of these incursions and its critical position over the assassination of Sayyid Qutb by the Egyptian regime (1966),[28] Boumediènne took this opportunity to suspend the work of this association (23rd September 1966) before finally banning it less than four years later (1970).

The third challenge was spearheaded by Islamic scholars and preachers who fought for their intellectual independence refusing to work for 'state Islam' and striving instead to promote their reformist ideas. The most prominent figure during the early years of independent Algeria (under Ben Bella's rule) was Bachir Ibrahimi (who served as leader of the *'ulamā'* after the death of Ben Bādīs). He was very critical of the ideological and programmatic choices made by the new republic and condemned them as a clear deviation from the principles for which over one million Algerians were martyred. In a letter to Ben Bella on 16 April 1964 he condemned such choices and wrote:

> Our rulers do not seem to understand that our people aspire foremost to unity, peace and prosperity and that the theoretical foundations guiding their [the rulers'] work should reflect our Arab and Islamic roots and should not be drawn from foreign doctrines.

Following this, he urged Ben Bella and his government to base their system on *shūrā* (consultation) and that they should strive for building a just and equitable polity. For this letter, Shaykh Ibrahimi was sentenced to house arrest until he died in his home on 21 May 1965.[29] After his death other religious scholars like Larbaoui, Sahnoun and Soltani carried on with this brand of oppositional Islam. Until his death, Abdelatif Soltani was the most virulent critic of the secularist policies of the successive Algerian presidents. He published a book in Morocco, in 1974, entitled *al-Mazdakīyya hīya aṣl al-ishtirākīyya* ('Mazdakism is the source of socialism'). This was a strong critique of the 'révolution socialiste' that was initiated by Boumediènne in 1971 and that sought the construction of a socialist Algeria. It also attacked the 'révolution culturelle' on the basis that it wanted to corrupt public morals by allowing the free-mixing of the sexes, the legal consumption of alcohol, and the lack of consideration for Islam by intellectual figures (particularly the writer Kateb Yacine and the feminist Fadhila Merabet) who were known for their ideological association with the regime. Abdelatif Soltani had a reputation for truculent rhetoric and staunch activism that cost him several dismissals from his job as a preacher under both Ben Bella and Boumediènne.

Shaykh Soltani was not only involved in the debates and intellectual confrontations over legislation on family, Arabization or the place of Islam in the institutional framework of independent Algeria, but he even co-led (with Sahnoun and Abbassi Madani) the November 1982 mass-rally and Friday Prayer at the Central Faculty of the University of Algiers.[30] This was seen by the Chadli regime as a serious test of its political determination not to allow any political opposition or challenge to its monopoly on Islam as a primary source of political legitimacy. This rally was organized after confrontations took place between leftist and Muslim students over student committees in campuses and over the question of the mosques of the halls of residence. The bloody confrontation at the Ben Aknoun hall of residence in early November that led to the death of one student (Kamal Amzal) and the arrest of several students[31] precipitated this event, which was significant for several reasons: firstly, it was a clear test of the regime's resilience when it was itself undergoing constant transformations reflecting the intra-regime power politics that were generated when Chadli tried to establish his authority at the expense of the old guard. Secondly, it marked the transformation of the Islamic strategy from one of clandestinity to semi-clandestinity, since it crowned the signatories (Soltani, Sahnoun, and Abbassi) of the 'Communiqué of Advice' as the collegial leadership of this movement. Finally, it issued a fourteen point communiqué that called for a wide-ranging programme of Islamization of society, covering such areas as the legal system, education, the economy, as well as professional ethics. It also called on the authorities to ensure public liberties and requested the opening of all closed mosques and prayer rooms in the educational sectors. Some of these points were endorsed by the regime. The best example is the promulgation of the 1984 family code which was essentially drawn from the *Sharīʿa*.

These events demonstrated once more the role played by university students not only in Islamic militancy but also in the historical development of the Islamic movement itself. In fact, in the 1960s (under Bennabi[32]) and 1970s university students spearheaded this tendency, at least amongst the youth, and challenged the influence of the communists (*Parti d'Avant Garde Socialiste*, PAGS[33]) in the highly sensitive sector of education.

The success of this event caused the regime to react quickly by arresting this new *de facto* leadership. Abbassi Madani remained in prison, while both Soltani (now eighty two years of age) and Sahnoun (seventy three years old) were released eight days later and put under house arrest.[34] Soltani remained under these restrictions until his death in March 1984. His funeral turned into another landmark in the development of the Algerian Islamic movement by bringing together tens of thousands of people, despite the media black-out on his death. This was the 'largest Islamist mobilization of the clandestine period ...'[35]

After the death of Soltani, Shaykh Ahmed Sahnoun became the most prominent Islamic leader in Algeria, partly because of his seniority as an Islamic scholar and partly because he had lived through and contributed to all the important phases of the Islamic movement, particularly after 1962. He founded in 1988 the *Islamic Propagation League (Rābiṭa al-Daʿwa al-Islāmīyya)* that brought together the majority of active Islamic groups and rallied around its project, for a period, the different strands of Algerian political Islam (Algerianists, the Muslim Brothers, the *Salafis* and the radicals). This league was apolitical and only reluctantly supported the creation of an Islamist party following the political quake of October 1988 that forced the regime to concede to political reforms based on pluralism and an unprecedented recognition of individual and public freedoms unseen in the Arab world.

Several political tendencies took advantage of this opening, which coincided with the lethargy of the regime and its unwillingness to repeat the October 1988 repression which had caused the death of over five hundred civilians in only five days of violence, to establish political parties even before the law regulating political associations was promulgated.[36] The Islamic tendency was no exception. This tendency was officially recognized by the Chadli regime as the major focal point of opposition in Algeria in view of the role it had played in stabilizing and calming the situation during the October events. Furthermore, Chadli and his regime officially recognized the leadership of this tendency when he received in his office (10th October) Ahmed Sahnoun, Abbassi Madani, Ali Belhadj, and Mahfoud Nahnah.

The *Front Islamique du Salut* (Islamic Salvation Front) was created in March 1989 and legalized in September 1989. It was soon to become the largest[37] and most active political party in Algeria. It was from the beginning an amalgam of different currents of political thought within the broader Islamic tendency. Although these currents converged on the ultimate goal (the establishment of an Islamic state) they diverged on both the political programme and the proposed strategy of action.[38] The FIS was a real mass party with a bicephalous leadership consisting of Abbassi Madani as President and Speaker, and Ali Belhadj as Deputy President. Madani is known as an intellectual – moderate, pragmatic, and politically experienced; Belhadj – as charismatic, young, confident in public speaking, and popular among the disenfranchized youth, particularly because of his uncompromising (and often not so prudent) attacks on the regime. This leadership is assisted by an executive and a sovereign Consultative

Council (*Majlis al-Shūrā*).

The FIS was able, from its outset, to capitalize on the long history of the Islamic movement by bringing under its control a large network of mosques and charitable and religious associations that were to serve as bases for the local and regional establishment of its national representation. It also managed to head-hunt most of the people engaged in *daʿwa*, or religious propaganda. Therefore it not only strengthened itself logistically but also enriched its 'ideological machine' with eloquent and competent people capable of converting more people to its political vision and platform of action.

The FIS established a dual strategy combining conciliation and aggressiveness. It used a double language that appealed both to a segment of the intelligentsia and a majority of the population. It attacked the state bureaucracy – its corruption and nepotism – and the spread of un-Islamic practices, and focused on social welfare through acts of national solidarity and large political demonstrations to force the regime to consider some Islamist perceptions on matters of national concern.[39] This multidimensional strategy and the strong organization that the FIS managed to build, in a short period of time, combined with the willingness of the population to break with the existing corrupt system and the inability of other parties to sell their ideas to the population. All of this gave the FIS a golden opportunity to take part in, and win, the first democratic local and regional elections in June 1990. In these elections the FIS won a landslide victory, capturing all the large and medium size cities. Sociologically, it gained cross-class electoral support[40] from businessmen, intellectuals, workers, the unemployed, women, and even the armed forces. These elections, on the other hand, discredited the ruling party (FLN) and demonstrated the weakness of the other parties in the absence of the second oldest party (the FFS, *Front des Forces Socialistes*).[41]

The FIS gained control of Algiers, Oran, Constantine, Tlemcen, Annaba, Setif, Guelma; the only major city it failed to win was Tizi-Ouzou (the biggest city of Kabylia) that fell under the control of the Kabylia-based party, the RCD. The south of Algeria, which is traditionally conservative, saved the face of the FLN which preserved a large number of seats. The FIS took control of 32 regional assemblies (APW, *Assemblée Populaire de Wilaya*) out of 48, and 853 out of the 1539 of the local councils (APC, *Assemblée Populaire Communale*).

Table 1: Results of the June 1990 Local and Regional Elections.

Political Affiliation	APC number of seats	%	APW number of seats	%
FLN	4799	36,60	667	35,61
PSD	65	0,50	6	0,36
PAGS	10	0,08	1	0,05
RCD	623	4,75	55	2,94
PNSD	134	1,02	8	0,43
FIS	5987	45,66	1031	55,04
PRA	61	0,46	4	0,21
PSL	5	0,004	2	0,11
PAHC				
PUAID	2	0,01		
INDEPENDENT CANDIDATES	1427	10,88	99	5,29

Burgat (Fr.): 'La mobilization Islamiste et les elections algériennes du 12 Juin 1990', in *Maghreb-Machrek*, No 129, July-September 1990, p. 7.

This success had several consequences. Firstly, the FIS electorate and the people in general began pressing for the immediate resolution of their social problems (most notably housing and unemployment) as promised by the FIS during its electoral campaign. Secondly, the management of the councils under the control of the FIS proved that the choice of candidates from amongst preachers and people without any managerial skills was politically risky and even disastrous. The FIS soon, however, managed to understand this problem and tried to alleviate it by organizing 'working meetings' for the new councillors. Thirdly, other branches of the Islamic tendency that refused to join the FIS soon realized that the best way of achieving both their personal ambitions and promoting their ideals was through open political participation by creating new parties. Nahnah was the first to move in this direction; first, he tried to undermine both the structural and popular bases of the FIS by calling for a meeting of all Islamic organizations. This was held on 20th September 1990 and attended by over 300 Islamic associations and groups, some key personalities as well as minor parties.[42] Encouraged by the relative success of this event, and driven by his persistent aspiration to lead the Islamic movement, Nahnah established, in December 1990, the *Movement of the Islamic Society*, or *Hamas*. This further divided the Islamic tendency rather than strengthening it. Djabbalah soon followed suit by creating *Nahda* (December 1990).

Finally, the regime understood the fact that it had made a serious political miscalculation by underestimating the real strength and potential mobilising power of the FIS. It tried, however, to undermine the credibility of the party by taking away the major prerogatives held by both the local and regional councils, especially those relating to the distribution of flats and land for construction. Moreover, the new elected bodies were confronted by a lack of cooperation from the designated *walis* (or regional governors). The last straw that led to a confrontation between the two sides was the promulgation of a new electoral law in the spring of 1991 that was specially tailored by the FLN-dominated National Assembly to maintain its control on this legislative body. This law led to strong acts of protest by several political parties, but it was the FIS that was set to lose most, and so decided, after the failure of all its contacts with the authorities, to launch what was termed a 'political strike'; in actual fact it turned out to be a failed attempt at civil disobedience that was organized only at Abbassi Madani's insistence.[43] This action was a serious miscalculation by the FIS; the regime and part of the army leadership were craving for such a mistake in order to restore their waning authority and to preserve their threatened privileges. After starting as peaceful sit-ins in public places (23rd May 1991), these turned bloody after the beginning of June. The bloodshed led to the dismissal of Hamrouche as head of government and his replacement by Ghozali, who promised to hold the legislative elections before the end of 1991 and to revise the electoral law. A state of siege was also declared on 5th June which brought the army back openly into politics. A vehement policy of repression followed. The leaders of the FIS were arrested on 29th June and thousands of known FIS activists were also arrested and detained, a curfew was introduced, and torture was widely applied. The regime wanted, through these concerted actions, to destabilize the organization of the FIS, weaken its unity and exploit the existing differences among its various components. This strategy had two objectives: the first was to find a more conciliatory leadership for the FIS, in order finally to domesticate it politically; the second was to avoid the emergence of any new party that would have an over-all majority in the National Assembly. In fact, this repression had two consequences for the FIS: the first was the disillusionment of the radical fringes of the FIS with the political 'game' and the subsequent decision to start organizing for armed insurgency;[44] the second was the emergence of a new political leadership after the Batna Conference of the party in August. This Conference dismissed several members of the *Majlis al-Shūrā* and elected Hachani as an interim President while maintaining both Abbassi and Belhadj in their posts. This new leadership was to prove in the following months, despite systematic repression, its political ingenuity, resourcefulness, and organizational inventiveness.

In fact, nobody was expecting a second landslide victory by the FIS given the systematic repression and concentrated attempts at destabilization to which it was subjected, the creation of new Islamist parties (*Hamas* and the *Movement of the Islamic Renaissance* or *Nahda*) and the consistent anti-FIS attacks by a large part of the media. The authorities were predicting that a maximum 25% of seats[45] would be obtained by the FIS at these first democratic legislative elections in independent Algeria. The results of these elections demonstrated once more two strong realities: first, the determination of a large section of the population to be rid of the regime and establish an Islamically-oriented polity. Second, it showed how much the regime was unprepared for political change and how isolated it was within a society that was changing very quickly.

In the elections themselves, the FIS won 188 seats in the first round (231 out of 430 seats were contested in the first round), followed by the FFS (25), the FLN (15) and three seats were won by independent candidates.There was no doubt that the FIS was set to win the second round, given the fact that it was the hot favourite for at least 177 of the remaining 199 seats. Algeria was on the verge of democratically electing the first pluralist assembly that would almost certainly yield an Islamist majority in government.

Table 2: Results of the First round of the legislative elections (26 December 1992)

Parties	% seats	Seats	Votes obtained
RCD	0	0	200,267
FIS	43,72	188	3,260 359
FLN	3,72	15	1,613 507
FFS	5,81	25	510 661
PRA	0	0	67 828
MDA	0	0	135 882
HAMAS	0	0	368 697

Lamchichi (A.): *L'Islamisme en Algérie*, l'Harmattan, Paris, 1992, p.83.

Such a prospect alarmed a cross-section of the *nomenklatura* and some associations, as well as some parties such as the PAGS and the RCD. The latter was unable to win even a single seat in its stronghold (Kabylia) and even its leader (Said Sadi) was ousted during the first round in his home town, Tizi Ouzou. Sadi called both for the cancellation of these elections by the army, and also for civil disobedience.[46] In the meantime, the leadership of the army (preeminently Defence Minister General Khaled Nezzar and Interior Minister Larbi Belkheir[47]) was preparing a constitutional takeover and the dismissal of Chadli in order to create a political and constitutional vacuum that could only be filled by a new presidential body.[48] This happened on 11th January 1992 when Chadli announced his resignation while the President of the Constitutional Council refused (or was forced to refuse) to assume his responsibilities as a constitutional interim president. This brought to the fore the High Council for Security, a consultative body with no executive powers. This council cancelled the elections, established a High Committee of State composed of five people and presided over by a veteran of the War of Liberation (Mohammed Boudiaf) living in exile (in Morocco) since the 1960s. Boudiaf was used, as a war hero, to give some historical legitimacy to the coup and to assume the responsibility of the decisions that were to be taken by the army-backed regime. These started with the promulgation of the 'state of emergency', the imprisonment of Hachani, the internment of tens of thousands of Islamists in concentration camps in the Sahara, the banning of the FIS, and the promulgation of highly restrictive legislation on individual and public freedoms.

The cancellation of these elections and the repression that followed had three consequences: firstly, it unleashed the radicals, hitherto contained within the complex framework of the FIS, propelling them to a general insurrection against the state. Secondly, the FIS was forced into clandestine work. It established two complementary leaderships, one internal and clandestine and the other external[49] (led by Rabah Kebir, who lives in exile in Germany). Thirdly, it put the country in a real state of civil strife that has cost more than 70,000 lives so far – a virtual civil war, that was precipitated just for the sake of saving the interests of the ruling minority.

The FIS has matured politically. Its coalition, in 1995, with seven other parties of the opposition against the regime, and its acceptance of all the rules of democracy (as outlined by the National Contract[50] signed in Rome in January 1995), as well as the different conciliatory gestures made towards the regime, are clear signs of such maturation.

There are two other major Islamist parties in Algeria, both subscribing to the *Ikhwān* current (The Muslim Brotherhood). One was within the framework established in Rome (*Nahda*); and the other

(*Hamas*) is participating in the institutions of the current regime, its leader (Mahfoud Nahnah) having stood as a candidate in the presidential elections, obtaining over 25% of the votes despite the elitist character of *Hamas* and the unpopularity of its leader among Islamists. This movement is represented in the current government with Aboujara Soltani as a junior minister for fisheries. Both parties signed on 15th August 1996 the 'Platform for National Entente' which was initiated by the presidency. The decision to sign this document, at least as far as *Nahda* is concerned, was motivated by reasons of *realpolitik* because several anti-Islamists were pressing for the outlawing of Islamist parties, in light of the fact that the presidential elections of the previous November had partially resolved the regime's problem of legitimacy. The solution was to accept a political domestication of these parties and their transformation into quasi-Social Democratic parties instead of facing the risk of a constitutional dismissal from open political practice.

THE POST-COUP STRATEGY OF THE REGIME

In order to avoid the Islamization of Algerian politics by the FIS after its victory in the first round of the 1991 general elections, and in order to secure their own interests and that of the *nomenklatura*, the army cancelled these elections and adopted a multi-dimensional (and gradual) strategy for the uprooting of the FIS as a political and social force. This zero-sum game strategy contained several sub-strategies: repressive and political, social and economic, legal and institutional, religious and military.

Politically, after the cancellation of the elections, the army nominated a five-man presidential body (the High Committee of State) to rule over the country until the end of 1993. This committee tried to reshape the political map of the country in order to enforce a universal resignation to the *fait accompli*. It banned the FIS, dissolved the local and regional councils it controlled, created a makeshift parliament (*Conseil Consultatif National*, CCN) of sixty members with no powers, to be replaced two years later with a similar institution (*Conseil National de Transition*, CNT), engaged in several pseudo-dialogues to gain time and to force a solution that would ensure the continuation of the post-coup system. The rejection of the National Contract concluded in January 1995 by the opposition is a clear indication of these intentions. The organization of the presidential elections (November 1995), despite the refusal of the major parties (FLN, FFS, *Nahda*, etc.) to take part therein, is further evidence of such intentions.

On the socio-economic level, the regime (as all post-coup populist regimes) offered economic incentives to the population by importing more basic commodities and ending the chronic food shortages, promising improved housing and better living standards. However, the implementation of the IMF program (from April 1994) proved the lack of realism in such promises and showed that the socio-economic problems of the country are structural and long-term. The socio-economic situation of the country is worse now than it has ever been, and it is predicted to worsen by 1999 when Algeria will have to start repaying its debt.

The favoured dimension in this complex strategy, however, is repression. All international organizations dealing with human rights issues agree that Algeria has the worst record in this respect: systematic torture, extra-judicial killings by government death squads, detention without trial, and so on. The worst case of such detentions was the creation in 1992 of several concentration camps in the desert, hosting more than 10,000 men, over 3,000 of whom were medical doctors or people with PhDs from Western universities.[51]

These repressive measures were reinforced by new legislation, such as the creation of special anti-terrorist courts (September 1993) where even the lawyers representing alleged terrorists were not safe from prosecution. In fact, lawyers launched several strikes to defend their rights. These courts passed more than 1000 capital sentences before being abolished in 1995. The second piece of legislation, signed in 1993, was a new law on the media, dramatically limiting the freedom of the press. As a consequence, several journalists were given prison sentences and newspapers were suspended and at times even banned.

The strategy of the regime also involved an attempt to regain its control over Islam as a source of legitimation and to undermine the potential in Islam for establishing oppositional discourse. It took several decisions in this direction:

a) replacing independent imams by government ones,

b) dissolving mosque committees and replacing them by government civil servants,

c) encouraging popular Islam (Sufism) (*les confreries marabou-tiques*) both financially and by giving more media focus to their activities, and by stressing the positive role they played in maintaining the Islamicity of Algeria when it faced the colonial onslaught, and

d) importing 'enlightened Islam' from al-Azhar.[52] Dozens of Egyptian scholars and preachers were brought to Algeria in 1992 to correct all the 'religious deviations' caused by political Islam. The logic of the government is to combine brute force with apolitical Islam in order to re-establish its sole right to Islam as a source of legitimacy.

The final dimension of this complex strategy comprises a number of reforms in the military establishment and its adaptation to the conditions of social bifurcation. These could be summarized as follows:

a) the restructuring of the security forces with the creation of an anti-terrorist force (60,000 men), a para-military force, civilian militia, and the restructuring of the intelligence services;[53]

b) the adaptation of the armed forces to guerrilla warfare, involving the provision of appropriate resources, such as night-sight equipment and helicopters;

c) the adoption of an anti-terrorist strategy based on the Soviet concept of 'Dirty War' to achieve maximum gains through a combination of provocation by *agents provocateurs*, penetration by double-agents, and fabrication of evidence and disinformation. The objective of such tactics is not only gains in military terms but also in psychological terms: turning ordinary people against the insurgents, and one armed group against another (several GIA-AIS confrontations and even intra-GIA killings have in fact taken place).

This strategy is not one of containment but of eradication. It aims at the final eradication of the FIS and of the model that the FIS wanted to establish (an Islamic State). Even the two other major Islamist parties that remain legal have dropped this term (Islamic State) from their rhetoric and foresee Islam only as an intellectual reference point. Such an effort at eradication, however, is bound to fail because the regime has not been able to offer any viable alternative model to the one that preceded it (the Chadli regime) but has simply replaced it with a form of government that has produced more repression, more unemployment, less security, less welfare and a veritable bath of Algerian blood. Even the concepts of sovereignty and independence so dear to all Algerians have lost their meaning in the midst of constant foreign interference, both overt and covert. Some specialists are even foreseeing a possible internationalization of the conflict.[54]

Despite all the above mentioned efforts on the part of the regime, and all the support given the regime by Arab and western – particularly French – governments, Islamism remains a strong social and political force in Algeria. If repression has proven its inability to contain the growth of such a phenomenon, the regime now has to use ingenuity and its desire for survival to find the most effective ways of silencing terrorism and moderating Islamist discourse. Both camps ought to seek a working historical compromise at all levels (epistemological, political, and societal). Only a historical compromise by all Algerians (without exclusion) can get Algeria out of this bifurcation and bloody civil war which is causing such a serious haemorrhage that the very persistence of the nation is now placed in jeopardy.

NOTES

1. See A. Christelow, 'Algerian Islam in a time of transition: c.1890-c.1930', *The Maghreb Review*, Vol.8 (5-6), 1983, pp. 124-130; and A. Faouzi, 'Islam, réformisme et nationalisme dans la résistance à la colonisation française en Algérie (1830-1930)', *Social Compass*, Vol.25 (3-4), 1985, pp. 419-432.

2. M. Gadant, *Islam et nationalisme en Algérie d'après El-Moudjahid, organe central du FLN de 1956 à 1962*, Paris: l'Harmattan, 1988, pp. 21-

33.

3. A large number of Algerians refused to be drafted into the French Army to participate in the First World War against Germany which was an ally of the Ottoman Empire. They still believed in the legitimacy of the Ottoman Caliphate and thought it was un-Islamic to join non-believers in combating it, albeit indirectly.

4. A. Merad, *Le réformisme musulman en Algérie de 1925 à 1940*, Paris & la Haye: Mouton & Co., 1967, pp. 13-14.

5. M. Al-Ahnaf, B. Botiveau, F. Frégosi, *L'Algérie par ses islamistes*, Paris: Karthala, 1991.

6. On the impact of the Iranian revolution on the development of Algerian Islamism, see L. W. Deheuvels, 'Islam officiel et islam de contestation au Maghreb: l'Algérie et la révolution iranienne', in D. Chevalier (ed), *Renouvellements du Monde Arabe: 1952-1982*, Paris: Armand Colin, 1987, pp. 133-152.

7. J. T. Dahlburg, reporting for the *Los Angeles Times*, 5 August, 1996, p. 11: 'Algerian veterans the nucleus for mayhem: at the start of the country's Islamic uprising, returnees from the Afghan war were sources of military expertise. They argued that it was futile to try to take power by peaceful means.'

8. See the text *Hidāya Rabb al-ʿālamīn fī tabyīn uṣūl al-Salafiyyīn* ... (Guidance of the Lord of the Worlds on Clarification of the Principles of the Salafis) Algiers: GIA, 1996, by the 'emir' of the GIA, Abu Abderrahman Amin.

9. See Omar Abdelhakim's *Al-thawra al-jihādīyya fī sūrīya* (The Jihadi Revolution in Syria), no publisher, date or place are mentioned. It is worth noting the second part of the text entitled *Fikr wa Manhaj* ('Thought and Method').

10. J. P. Entelis, *Political Islam in the Maghreb: the non-violent dimension*, Congressional Testimony, U.S. Congress, House of Representatives, Committee on Foreign Affairs, Sub-Committee on Africa, Washington D.C., 28 September 1994.

11. Ibid.

12. Ibid.

13. For an exhaustive history of the MIA, refer to Yahia Abou

Zakaria, *Al-ḥaraka al-islāmīyya al-muṣālaḥa*, ('The Armed Islamic Movement') Beirut: Dār al-Maʿārif, 1993.

14. Entelis, op.cit.

15. Ibid.

16. *L'Express*, 16 November 1995, p. 22.

17. Entelis, op.cit.

18. Ibid.

19. *L'Express*, op.cit.

20. This group joined the GIA in May 1994 when the leader of the Algerianist tendency (Mohamed Said) joined the GIA's *Majlis al-shūrā* (Consultative Council).

21. *Compass*, 29 July 1996.

22. Zouabri comes from the Islamist stronghold of Boufarik, 25 kms to the south-west of Algiers.

23. They were led until July 1996 by Zitouni as their Emir while Mohamed Said served, until his assassination in November 1995, as a member of the GIA's Consultative Council.

24. *Maghreb Confidentiel*, 28 September 1995.

25. Entelis, op.cit.

26. Ibid.

27. Tidjani served as General Secretary of the University of Algiers (1962-1964) and as General Secretary of the Ministry of Religious Affairs (1965-1966).

28. *al-Qiyam* sent a letter to Gamal Abd al-Nasser in September 1966 pleading for the release of Sayyid Qutb shortly before he was killed.

29. Fawzi Ben el-Hashemi Oussedik: *Maḥaṭāṭ fī tārīkh al-ḥaraka al-islāmīyya al-jazā'irīyya* (Landmarks in the History of the Algerian Islamic Movement 1962-1988), Algiers: Intifada, 1992, pp. 13-24.

30. It was Abbassi Madani who called for this rally during a Friday sermon delivered at the Ibn Bādīs mosque in Kouba (Algiers) on 5 November 1982. This call was received with mixed feelings by other factions of the Islamic tendency. While it was rejected by the Algerianists, it was openly supported by Shaykh Ahmed Sahnoun on 7 November 1982. This approbation forced them to reconsider their

position and participate in this event.

31. Twenty nine students were arrested following this confrontation.

32. A. Khelladi: *Les Islamistes Algériens Face au Pouvoir*, Algiers: Editions Alfa, 1992.

33. The PAGS was the only party tolerated by the regime after 1967.

34. F. Burgat, W. Dowell: *The Islamic Movement in North Africa*, Center for Middle Eastern Studies, University of Texas at Austin, 1993, p. 264.

35. Ibid., p. 251.

36. Several tendencies started, after the popular endorsement of the new Constitution (on 23rd February 1989), to establish themselves as political organizations either as mass movements (FIS) or 'cadre parties' (*Rassemblement pour la Culture et la Démocratie*, RCD, and others). These new organizations were established before the law regulating their work was finally promulgated by the Popular National Assembly on 5th July 1989.

37. The leadership of the FIS claimed on numerous occasions, particularly during 1990 and 1991, that its membership was in excess of three million. This number seems to be exaggerated in view of the impossibility of gathering such a membership in less than two years of formal existence. Secondly, this number is not far from the votes obtained during the contested local and legislative elections. It is not normal that all the votes obtained are from an established membership.

38. It was primarily because of these strategic differences that the leadership of FIS was neither willing nor able to organize its Congress for fear of implosion.

39. The biggest such demonstration was the one on the Family Code (December 1989) that drew hundreds of thousands of women. It came as a response to the one held a week earlier by feminist associations calling for the revision of this legislation.

40. A. Lamchichi: *L'Islamisme en Algérie*, Paris: l'Harmattan, 1992, p. 264.

41. The FFS was established on 19th September 1963 by Hocine Ait Ahmed (a co-founder of the FLN and one of the forefathers of Algerian nationalism), Abdelhafid Yaha and Colonel Si Sadek. This party was banned after the 'Kabyle insurrection' in autumn 1963 and Ait Ahmed was imprisoned in early 1964 until his escape from prison in April 1966. He lived in Switzerland and Morocco until his return to Algeria after the re-legalization of his party on 20th November 1989. The FFS is a member of the Socialist Internationale and is strong mainly in Kabylia and parts of Algiers. The FFS decided not to take part in these local elections judging that the conditions there were unconducive to their success.

42. H. Roberts: 'A Trial of Strength: Algerian Islamism', in J. Piscatori (ed.) *Islamic Fundamentalism and the Gulf Crisis - The Fundamentalist Project*, American Academy of Arts and Sciences, 1991, p. 137.

43. According to several prominent members of the FIS, several leading figures of this party were opposed to such actions and warned Abbassi against the possible negative consequences. They believed that they were giving the regime a golden opportunity to launch actions against the FIS. They were soon proven right.

44. According to Aissa Khelladi ('Esquisse d'une géographie des groupes Islamistes en Algérie', *Herodote*, No. 77, 1995, pp. 28-29) the decision to prepare for an armed insurgency was taken in July 1991 at a meeting in the mountains of Lakhdaria (80 kms to the east of Algiers) by a number of people that participated in the first such insurgency with Bouyali and the MIA (1982-1987). The most prominent participants were Chabouti and Miliani. Despite agreeing on the need for an insurgency they disagreed on both tactics and strategy. While the former favoured the establishment of an organized army following the example of the National Liberation Army (1954-1962), the latter favoured urban guerrilla warfare, to be conducted by small groups.

45. This projection was on the basis of a study done by the 'Internal Politics Department' of the *Institut National Des Etudes et des Stratégies Globales* (INESG, a think-tank that works for the President's

office) in the autumn of 1991.

46. Lamchichi, op.cit., p. 84.

47. C. Migdalovitz: *Algeria: Four Years of Crisis*, Congressional Research Service – Report for Congress, Washington D.C., 1996, p. 84

48. For a good insight into the coup, see P. Dévoluy & M. Duteil, *La poudrière algérienne: Histoire secrète d'une révolution sous influence*, Paris: Calmann-Lévy, 1994.

49. According to a press release (reported by *al-Sharq al-Awsaṭ*, 10 February 1996) by the FIS Executive Committee overseas, signed by its president R. Kebir, the institutions of the FIS are:

1) the 'representative leadership' in prison: Abbassi and Belhadj;

2) the internal leadership led by Ali Djeddi, Abdelkader Boukhamkham, Kamal Guemmazi and Abdelkader Omar;

3) the *Islamic Salvation Army* (AIS) under the overall leadership of Madani Mezrag, and

4) the Executive Committee of the FIS overseas under the leadership of Rabah Kebir.

50. This National Contract was signed by seven Algerian parties (FIS, *Nahda*, FLN, FFS, MDA, the *Trotskyist Party of Workers*, and *Contemporary Muslim Algeria*) with diverging ideological colorations. These were joined by the *Algerian League for the Defence of Human Rights* (led by its president Ali Yahia Abdenour). This contract outlined the principles of democratic practice in Algeria and made some suggestions for the resolution of the crisis. The regime rejected it immediately and led a strong propaganda campaign against it by presenting it as an act of foreign interference in its internal affairs.

51. *The Rape of a Nation: the hidden face of Algeria*, Algerian Forum, Hoggar, 1995, pp. 10-14.

52. A. Rouadjaia: 'Le FIS est-il enterré? Al-Azhar au secours de l'Etat algérien', in *Esprit*, June 1993, pp. 94-103.

53. *Intelligence*, No.261, 27 March 1995, p. 65.

54. P. St. John: 'Insurgency, legitimacy and intervention in Algeria', *Commentary* (Canadian Security Intelligence Service), No.65, January 1996.

CHAPTER IV

THE ARMY IN ALGERIAN POLITICS AND GOVERNMENT

George Joffé

Independent Algeria was born in the crucible of the war of independence, between 1954 and 1962. It was the war which forged a spirit of national identity out of the disparate desires and loyalties of ten million Algerians, one million of whom died in the conflict.[1] For many years after independence, Algerian institutions and the ideology of the state bore the marks of this violent beginning and thus, not surprisingly, the Algerian army (*l'Armée Nationale Populaire* – ANP) has been intimately involved with political and national development. The role of the army in the political history of independent Algeria has been even more intimately involved in the development of the state than this would suggest, however, because of the specific way in which the state evolved immediately after the Evian Accords were signed in July 1962, particularly during the Boumediènne era. The intense inter-dependence of state and army has also been dramatically underlined by the way in which the crisis created by the interruption of the electoral process in January 1992 has evolved. Indeed, the future of Algeria today is as much a question of the intentions of the army leadership as it is a matter of the objectives of its political opponents, whether Islamist or secular.

THE ARMY AND THE WAR FOR INDEPENDENCE

The Algerian army was created on October 10, 1954 as the *Armée de Libération Nationale* (ALN)[2] by the revolutionary heads of the *wilāya*-s, the provincial divisions created by the *Front de Libération Nationale* (FLN) in which autonomous groups began the struggle for independence through guerrilla warfare against the French colonial administration and security forces. The very nature of the war, however, meant that the ALN remained little more than a title rather than an institutional reality, for the *wilāya* guerrilla groups bore the brunt of the armed struggle and tended to operate independently from each other and from any centralized command structure. As a result, on August 24, 1956, the ALN was re-organized during the First Soummam Conference in which the new *Conseil National de la Révolution Algérienne* (CNRA) – the ruling body of the FLN and the Revolution – defined the ALN as the armed vehicle of the Revolution but insisted that ultimate control of the Revolution should remain in the hands of a collegiate political leadership – the *Comité de Coordination et d'Execution* (CCE), which was eventually replaced by the *Gouvernement Provisoire de la République Algérienne* (GPRA) in September 1958. Yet, at the same time, the Conference recognized the fact that the *wilāya*-s would remain effectively independent of any central command structure by allowing strategic and tactical decisions made by the *wilāya* leadership inside Algeria to take priority over decisions made by the external army and political leadership.[3]

Thus, right at the beginning of the Algerian revolution, a duality developed within the structures of its armed forces that was to prove fatal some years later. Despite the intentions of the participants in the Soummam Conference which anticipated the eventual control of the guerrilla war by the ALN leadership, French strategy ensured that this did not happen. FLN military strategy had been predicated on a Chinese and Vietnamese blueprint (although it was popularly perceived in terms of a *jihād*) in which guerrilla warfare would pave the way for conventional warfare in which the mobility of the popular forces would out-manouevre the more heavily-armed forces of their opponent. As a result, the ALN was organized as *mujāhidīn* – regular armed forces – *musibilīn* – para-military auxiliaries recruited locally and designed to provide support for the regular forces – and *fidā'īn* – untrained non-combatant auxiliaries.[4] In reality, the 45,000-strong conventional regular armed forces, which had to be created outside the country in Morocco and Tunisia, were kept out of Algeria throughout the war by the creation of two electrified fences along the borders – the *Ligne Challe* and the *Ligne Morice*. The armed struggle, instead, devolved onto the guerrilla groups in the *wilāya*-s whose leaders thus became significant military leaders in their own right with no over-riding control from the army high command, based in Oujda (Morocco) under Colonel Houari Boumediènne. Even the highly effective ALN urban underground which terrorized the urban *colon*[5] community operated virtually autonomously.

At the same time, the FLN political structure became increasingly integrated into the military command structure marooned outside Algeria, with the military leadership being effectively in the commanding position,[6] so that, by 1962, a veritable military-dominated state-in-embryo existed abroad awaiting the opportunity to take over a country shattered by war.[7] It was, therefore, not surprising that the advent of Independence in July 1962 was immediately attended by a *coup d'état* in which the leaderships of the GPRA and the *wilāya* guerrilla forces were displaced by a coalition between the army leadership under Houari Boumediènne and one of the nine original leaders (*chefs historiques*) of the FLN, Ahmed Ben Bella, who had been captured by French forces in October 1956, just after the Soummam Conference, and held in prison until the end of the conflict. In effect, the Algerian revolution had been hijacked, in Thomas Hodgkin's words, by a 'military-bureaucratic oligarchy'.[8]

THE ARMY IN THE INDEPENDENT STATE

The first task facing Algeria's new rulers was to construct an effective administration and political institutions from the detritus of war. Ahmed Ben Bella, who was to provide the public face for the new regime, with the army leadership remaining in the background, was anxious to create a vanguard political party from the FLN as the vehicle for the integration of the new state. After having dispersed the remnants of the opposition to the original *coup*, he forced through the Algiers Charter during an FLN conference in April 1964. Although the Charter proclaimed a socialist option for the new Algerian state, this was also declared not to be at odds with Algeria's Arab and Islamic heritage and the FLN was to be the 'catalyst and motor' of the revolution.[9] There was, however, considerable resistance to Ben Bella's plan from his all-important backers in the army, led by the army commander, Houari Boumediènne.

The opposition was based on the fact that the new role for the FLN was seen as a challenge to the hegemony of the army over Algeria's political future – for the army was seen and saw itself as the guarantor of the Algerian Revolution. There were other objections, too. Some FLN activists believed that the secular and Marxist overtones of the Charter were unacceptable in a country where Islam had been the dominant cultural and socio-political theme during the war itself. They also feared that the revolution's commitment to an Arabic identity would be weakened, although here there were counter-arguments over the issue of Algeria's Berberophone population – 25 per cent of the total and far more heavily represented within the revolutionary elite than this demographic distribution would suggest. Other FLN activists also feared that the army officer corps, particularly the junior officer corps, was dominated by petty bourgeois sentiments, largely because of the way in which it had recruited, particularly towards the end of the armed struggle, which saw the FLN's socialist option as a threat to their vested interests.[10]

This opposition was to surface once again the following year, for by now Ben Bella, although he had defeated his political opponents, had failed to build a personal support-base within the new regime and his dependence on the army ran counter to their disagreements over the course the country was to take. Ben Bella, of course, was aware of the danger and after ensuring his control of the presidency by popular vote in 1963, he had begun to try to curb the untrammeled power of Boumediènne and his associates – the so-called 'Oujda Clan' – within the Army General Staff. Tahar Zbiri, a former *wilāya* chief, was appointed chief of the General Staff in October 1963 and then, in 1964, pro-Boumediènne ministers were forced from office, including Ahmed Medeghri, the interior minister, Ahmed Kaid at tourism and

Cherif Belkacem at the education portfolio. By 1965, of the original Oujda Clan only Boumediènne himself, with the defence portfolio, and Abdelaziz Bouteflika at foreign affairs were left in government. The final straw was the attempt by the president to create a popular militia force which, in the eyes of the ANP, would replace it as guardian of the state and the Revolution. On June 19, 1965, Ben Bella was ousted and a new Revolutionary Council, headed by Colonel Houari Boumediènne, took over Algeria.

The coup brought the army to the fore of government in Algeria. Although the Boumediènne regime was highly personalized and intensely bureaucratic, the key decisions up to Boumediènne's death in December 1978 were essentially taken by a coterie of senior army officers around the president, particularly after the Oujda Clan had been effectively disbanded by 1974. President Boumediènne incorporated the old *wilāya* guerrilla leaders into the new administration, using party and state patronage as a means of neutralising their hostility, whilst those, like Tahar Zbiri, who opposed him, were crushed in 1967. The new state structure abandoned the idea of the FLN as a vanguard party, depriving it of an independent power-base and turning it instead into a tool of government. A drive was introduced to create new political structures through popular local and regional assemblies under strong central control and the old 1963 constitution, together with the National Assembly, were abolished. In effect, Algeria became a state in which power was no longer institutionalized but was controlled by an unaccountable elite of bureaucrats, technocrats and army officers[11] – a *nomenklatura*, in other words.

It was only in 1976 that a new constitution was approved by referendum, after a long public debate designed to legitimize the policies of the Boumediènne regime. Yet the new constitution, whilst providing for a new Popular National Assembly (*Assemblé Populaire National* – APN) and theoretically making the FLN the guarantor of the revolution alongside the army, in reality strengthened the powers of the president by making him effectively independent of all potentially autonomous sources or groups holding power within the state.[12] Indeed, the FLN was even to be revived, albeit under indirect army control, by Colonel Mohamed Salah Yahyaoui, appointed as secretary-general in October 1977.[13] In addition, beyond this formal structure, real power in Algeria remained with those individuals who, by their association with the army, had created their own personal fiefs within the state or who, through their positions within the bureaucracy, were able to do the same through their control of the state capitalist system which the Boumedienne regime had created. Others in the technocratic elite sought similar opportunities, often in conjunction with their access into the private sector which still made up 30 per cent of the Algerian economy.[14] In short, control of real power inside Algeria remained informal and arbitrary, outside the scope of formal state institutions, whether new or old, with the army still playing a key role in economic and political life.

Boumedienne's death illustrated the importance of the army quite clearly, for it was the army leadership which designated his chosen successor who was then approved by the FLN before being elected by universal suffrage. The chosen, indeed sole, candidate was one of the army's most senior officers, Colonel Chadli Ben Djedid, who had been army commander in Oran. He had been a compromise candidate forced on the FLN by the army when the factions supporting the party's secretary-general (and army officer), Mohamed Yahyaoui, and the former foreign minister and Oujda Clan member, Abdelaziz Bouteflika, were deadlocked.[15] Chadli Ben Djedid was well-aware that there had to be change in Algeria and he opted for economic liberalization whilst trying to retain control over an increasingly unruly political scene. This was dominated by unrest amongst the Berberophone population after April 1980, which turned into demands for greater political freedom, and by increasing tensions with the country's nascent Islamist movements which had been repressed during the Boumedienne era but which began to play an increasingly significant role after 1984. Often the two strands of opposition to the regime were also opposed to each other, particularly in the context of a major debate over the Arabization of public life which began during the 1980s. The regime itself, however, continued to be dominated by the same division of power as before, between bureaucrats, technocrats, and the army – a feature which was intensified by the economic reforms introduced during the early 1980s.

Although the state capitalist option was not to be abandoned until 1987, when Algeria's foreign debt problems became insurmountable,[16] partly because of the collapse of world oil prices in the previous year, economic liberalization, designed to improve consumer supply, began in the early 1980s. This, in turn, led to the growth of a new bourgeoisie which exploited the opportunities offered, particularly in agricultural goods and finished consumer products. Often its members came from the bureaucratic and technocratic elite who were able to exploit the opportunities presented by their positions for personal gain. Even if they were far less powerful or omnipresent than popular myth soon suggested, they became typified by and were parodied as the *milliardaires de légumes* – the vegetable millionaires. They represented the growing economic differentiation in Algerian society that ran directly counter to the principles of the Revolution and the ideals of the 'historic FLN'.[17] Insofar as they also operated outside legal control, because of their elite status, they were perceived to be – and often, indeed, were – a corrupt mafia sapping at the ideals of the Revolution.

Alongside this economic differentiation grew up another, based on cultural paradigms. Algerians increasingly saw themselves divided into a Francophone elite, cosmopolitan, secular, and dependent on its links to Europe through France and the French language – to which Berberophone groups were, in part, linked – and the mass of the population in *l'Algérie profonde* – Muslim, Arabophone, conscious of its identity with the Arabic and Islamic worlds, and resentful of its perceived exploitation by government and elite alike. Its claims to sovereign authenticity were, it is true, disputed by Berberophone Kabylia and the Chaouia which saw themselves as the true repositories of Algeria's national cultural heritage, but both claimants could agree that the French dimension was alien to this sense of national identity, however expressed. Thus, in the popular mind, the elite, already alienated by its economic advantage and seen as the *mafia*, was now further alienated by its identification with European culture through links with the French. Popular mythology here created a shadowy *Hizb Fransa* – the party of France – which was supposed to penetrate, through the elite, into economic and political life and allow the former colonial power to re-assert its control on the independent state.

The Berber-Arab-French split was also replicated within the army leadership where, in the mid-1980s, a major dispute brewed over the future structure of Algeria's armed forces. The old pattern of a popular army was abandoned in favour of a conventional force along typical Western lines, which was favoured by the increasingly influential school of senior officers educated in France or with early military experience in the French army. They, after all, were the second generation since the Revolution, and had not had leading roles during the struggle for Independence but had come to prominence after it and, in many cases indeed, after the end of the Boumediènne era as well. The older, populist vision was supported by officers who had originally received their training in the Soviet Union or in the Arab world and were known contemptuously as graduates from the 'Baghdad Artillery School'. As the economic and social crises intensified during the 1980s, the army's background role as guarantor and arbiter of political power became increasingly open to criticism, particularly as the proposed reforms began to threaten its traditional power-bases. The Francophone elements within its leadership became increasingly significant, for they were most familiar with, and tolerant of, the types of reforms which were being considered and which would profoundly undermine the populist and nationalist assumptions on which Algeria had been constructed, particularly by the Boumediènne regime.

The gathering crisis erupted in October 1988, when popular anger at economic failure and lack of political participation exploded into a countrywide spate of rioting which forced radical political change. The army was brought in to suppress the violence and incurred particular odium for the techniques it used. As a result, when a new constitution was approved – Algeria's third – in 1989, the army's role was down-graded, from the obligation both to safeguard the country's frontiers and the revolution, to the more familiar constitutional duty of guaranteeing national unity and sovereignty.[18] Shortly thereafter the army also withdrew from all political roles and positions, suggesting that, for the first time since 1962, the presidency, now controlling a multi-party political system, had freed itself from the political control of the army as well. Given its continued role within the informal and now increasingly corrupt structure of arbitrary power in Algeria, however, this retreat was to prove to be more illusory than real.[19]

THE ARMY RETURNS TO POWER

There is little doubt that it was the rise of the Islamist movements in Algeria that provoked the army's return to the political centre stage. Its retreat had been predicated on an assumption that Chadli ben Djedid could exploit the new multi-party system to re-establish presidential control of the political process by dominating the political arena and mediating between the parties, amongst which the FLN would have a special, revitalized, and central role.[20] The FIS (*Front Islamique du Salut* – *Jabḥa Islāmīyya li'l-Inqāth*), in this vision, would then become only one amongst several parties contesting for the loyalties of Algerian Muslims. By June 1990, it was evident that this attempt at reconstructing the Algerian political scene was failing. The victory of the FIS in the municipal elections was evidence enough of the failure. The army, however, agreed to allow the presidency to resume its experiment, provided that it accepted a military return to the political arena. The price was the appointment of General Khalid Nezzar, the senior army officer, as defence minister – the first time that this had occurred since independence.

The presidential initiative, however, continued to fail, largely because of a struggle for control within the FLN itself, between the new reformist wing, led by the former prime minister, Mouloud Hamrouche, and his aide, the former economics minister, Ghazi Hidouci, and the nationalist old guard who were not prepared to abandon the essential popularist and socialist tenets of FLN ideology.

A year later, in the run-up to legislative elections, FIS protests at what was perceived to be a biased electoral law resulted in strikes and demonstrations. On this occasion, the army took matters into its own hands and arrested the FIS leadership. It now forced the president to appoint a new interior minister, General Larbi Belkhair. There were even rumours rife in Algiers that there was also a plan to replace the president by one of the few remaining *chefs historiques* of the revolutionary period, Mohamed Boudiaf, who had gone into exile in Morocco after an abortive attempt to unseat Ahmed Ben Bella in 1964.

The two military appointments in government were significant in several ways. Firstly, the army was now overtly in charge of security in ways that had never been the case before, thus diminishing presidential autonomy. Secondly, both officers in government were from the Francophone component of the senior officer corps, had good contacts in France, and rejected the old concept of the army as an instrument of popular resistance, seeing it instead within the modern European and American concept of conventional warfare. Thirdly, as part of the Francophone tradition, they were also popularly seen as linked to the *nomenklatura*, and through this to the *Hizb Fransa* with its associations with the shadowy *mafia*. Their appointments, as it were, helped to draw the battle lines, so that the presidential project of incorporating the FIS as an element – but not the dominant element – in the multi-party political scene, became ever more unrealistic as the regime itself, by implication, became increasingly associated in the popular mind with the mythical *Hizb Fransa*, corruption, and the *mafia*.

The lack of presidential realism was underlined by the December 1991 legislative elections in which the FIS, although seeing its vote decline in absolute and relative terms, still won an overwhelming victory.[21] The army leadership was not prepared to tolerate the FIS forming a government in which its own prerogatives and privileges would be threatened, not to speak of the basic assumptions which had governed the Algerian state since its inception. Nor was it prepared to tolerate further political experiments by a regime in which it no longer had confidence. As a result, Chadli Ben Djedid was replaced by a collegiate army-dominated leadership which then invited Mohamed Boudiaf to return as its head. There is little doubt that the army's intention was to create a formal collegiate presidency behind which it would oversee government, for both Khalid Nezzar and Larbi Belkhair retained their government posts and were joined in the legitimating transitional body by the army chief-of-staff, Abelmalek Guennaizia, whilst Khalid Nezzar also joined the new collegiate presidency, now headed by Mohamed Boudiaf.

The new administration was predicated on the assumption that Mohamed Boudiaf would accept a role as titular president, rather than as a genuine executive outside the collegiate context. It was also based on the assumption that the FIS could be eradicated from the political arena, so that a modified democratic system – one better controlled by the new presidential institution – could be introduced and the elections repeated without the FIS taking part but with better domesticated Islamist movements being involved. Mr Boudiaf, however, realized that the old-style Algerian regime had completely lost popular credibility and that a new popular consensus would have to be achieved if a modified version of it were to be revived, thus preserving the continuity of the revolutionary ideal of a state based on popular sovereignty. His attempts to create a mass movement to achieve this end during the first six months of 1992 inevitably touched on the areas of privilege enjoyed by the Algerian *nomenklatura* and its army patrons connected to the *Hizb Fransa*. His assassination, in June 1992, although blamed on Islamist influence within his own presidential guard, was popularly credited to dissident elements within the *securité militaire*. Direct responsibility was laid at the door of the interior minister, Larbi Belkhair, who left office as a result. The army still remained in charge and now turned to one of the old FLN grandees, Belaid Abdesslam, who had been a senior economics minister under Houari Boumedienne, to form a new government in order to resolve Algeria's economic crisis as a precursor to a new political initiative.

His failure, in August 1993, also highlighted a growing split within the army leadership about how the political crisis should now be addressed. By this time, a widespread armed Islamist resistance to the regime had developed in which there were two discernible strands – the *Groupe Islamique Armé* (GIA), which hailed from the old *Afghaniste* faction of the FIS, and the wider-based *Mouvement Islamique Armé* (MIA), soon to become the *Armée Islamique du Salut* (AIS). Within the army leadership, two similar divisions had also developed – one group, the so-called *conciliateurs*, sought to negotiate with the FIS and thus find a compromise solution to the crisis; the other, the *éradicateurs*, saw no grounds for compromise at all and argued for outright repression. The *conciliateurs* were generally close to the Arabophone wing of the army leadership; the *éradicateurs* tended to be drawn from the ranks of the modernist Francophone leadership.[22] The most senior levels of the leadership around Khalid Nezzar who was by then ill, seemed to have been nonplussed by their failure to find a viable way forward and were beginning to be displaced by their subordinates.

The new approach was heralded by the assassination of the last remaining figure from the previous era, Kasdi Merbah, a former head of intelligence and prime minister, who had been calling for reconciliation and had been seen as a possible successor to Belaid Abdesslam. His death, also officially attributed to Islamist violence, was almost certainly the work of *sécurité militaire* dissidents who were determined to avoid any possibility of a weakening of the policy of outright repression. This approach was also supported by the secular elite and by some Berber nationalists, particularly those associated with Said Saadi's *Rassemblement constitutionel et démocratique* (RCD), although opposed by virtually every other political party and by most strands of popular opinion as well. By this time, the *securité militaire* dissidents also appeared to have penetrated elements of the GIA whose increasingly spectacular terrorist attacks did far more to justify the regime's criticism of the Islamist movement as a whole than they ever did to discredit the regime itself.

END GAME?

The growing tensions within the army leadership over the way forward reflected the habitual struggle within government in Algeria over policy options. The government was traditionally factionalized, such that conflict was not only caused by differing attitudes towards objectives but was also the mode by which such differences would eventually be resolved. The result has been that, over the past three years, there has been a vicious tussle within the regime over what should be done between *éradicateurs* and *conciliateurs* which has centred around the role and policies of the man who became president in early 1994, Liamine Zerouel. He is a former army general who retired during the latter years of the Chadli Ben Djedid regime because he disagreed with presidential support for the modernization of the army along conventional Western lines. He was trained in Iraq and was an original member of the FLN struggle against France. His re-introduction to power, first as defence minister in August 1993 and then as president in February 1994, was among the last acts of Khalid Nezzar, who later became a presidential adviser until his retirement earlier this year. His appointment was designed to provide a means for trying the option of a negotiated solution to the Algerian crisis, in which the *éradicateurs* would acquiesce.

In fact, although the negotiating option was tried during 1994, it was continually frustrated by the *éradicateur* faction, led by Generals Lamari, Touati and Mediène. As a result, the Algerian crisis has been increasingly internalized within the regime as each faction tries different options to outwit its opponents. In the meantime, the wider crisis has been largely ignored or down-played as the faction struggle within the regime continues. To some extent, the Algerian authorities have been aided in this approach by the attitudes of their foreign backers, particularly in France after the GIA-inspired bombing campaign last year.

The presidential election last November was one such option, although it was also intended to cut through the complexities of negotiation and the support offered by the officially recognized political parties to FIS participation in a resolution to the crisis.[23] Now the regime is attempting to exclude the FIS from all negotiation by trying to reconstruct the political arena in a pattern similar to that originally proposed by Chadli Ben Djedid in 1989, so that the presidency dominates the political parties, with the FLN resuscitated as a presidential party in its own right. In short, the presidency, despite its *conciliateur* reputation, has brought part, at least, of the *éradicateur* approach to a resolution of the crisis. At the same time, President Zerouel, aided by his adviser, Mohamed Bitchine, is trying to winkle the leading *éradicateurs* out of power so that he can eventually control the army leadership, in a repeat of the pattern first introduced by President Boumediènne in 1965, after the Revolution. The reality is, however, that, in the end, the army will have to come to terms with its Islamist opponents, if a real solution to the crisis is to be found. No doubt, it cannot be beaten by them, but it also knows it cannot beat them. Perhaps President Zerouel intends to come to just such a compromise with the Islamists, once he has established control over the factions within the army leadership itself, although his latest plans do not encourage much hope. This time, however, the army leadership will have to face the bleak consequences of its own failure as the guardian of Algeria's failed revolution.∾

NOTES

1. Algeria's population during the war is extremely difficult to establish. The 1996 census suggested that the population then was 11.8 million, with a growth rate of 3.3 per cent per year, and the earlier French censuses during the colonial period were inaccurate. (See R. Nyrop, (ed), *Area Handbook for Algeria*, Washington: American University, 1972, pp. 85-86; and R. Nyrop (ed), *Algeria: a country study*, Washington: American University, 1979, p. 73.) Deaths during the conflict were put at 350,000, according to French army sources and at one million by the post-Independence Algerian authorities. (Ibid. p. 74; and A. Horne, *A Savage War of Peace: Algeria 1954-1962*, London: Penguin, 1977, p. 358.)

2. It became the *Armée Nationale Populaire* (ANP) at the end of the war.

3. See E. O'Ballance, *The Algerian Insurrection: 1954-1962*, London: Faber & Faber, 1967, pp. 70-75; and A. Humbaraci, *Algeria: a Revolution That Failed*, London: Pall Mall, 1966, pp. 63-65.

4. O'Ballance, op. cit., p. 74.

5. Colon: French settler colonialist, also known as the *pieds noirs*.

6. W. Quandt, *Revolution and Political Leadership: 1954-1968*, Cambridge - USA: MIT Press, 1969, pp. 138-140.

7. R. Tlemcani, *State and Revolution in Algeria*, London: Zed, 1986, pp. 64-65.

8. Ibid., p.62.

9. J. Ruedy, *Modern Algeria: the Origins and Development of a Nation*, Indianapolis: Indiania University Press, 1992, pp. 204-5.

10. Ibid., pp. 204-5. Colonel Boumediènne had been prepared to integrate Algerians who had served in the French army into the new ANP which replaced the ALN at Independence in 1962, simply for the sake of creating an effective military machine. In July 1964, he stated:
'The revolution having entrusted me with the task of building an army, I do this with those who are the most capable. I prefer to work with Algerians, however late they may have joined our revolution, rather than with foreign experts.'
It was officers from this group which formed the basis of the Army General Staff and thus had considerable influence over policy formulation. (Humbaraci, op. cit., p. 227.)

11. Ruedy, op. cit., p. 209.

12. J. Leca & C. Vatin, 'Le système politique algérien (1976-78). Idéologie, institution, et changement social', in Anon (1979), *Développement politiques au Maghreb. Aménagements institutionels et processus électoraux*, Paris: CNRS, 1979, pp. 27-8.

13. H. Roberts, 'The politics of Algerian socialism', in R. Lawless & A. Findlay, *North Africa*, London: Croom Helm, 1984, p. 30.

14. H. Roberts, 'The Algerian Bureaucracy', in T. Asad & R. Owen *The Middle East*, London: Macmillan, 1983, pp. 95-114.

15. Ruedy, op. cit., p. 232.

16. Ibid., p. 242.

17. The FLN during its heroic period of struggle against France was increasingly seen in popular mythology as the repository of Algeria's revolutionary legitimacy after the Ben Bella coup in 1962. As the historic FLN it was contrasted with the subordinated mass party

structure exploited by both the Boumedienne and Ben Djedid regimes as a means of ensuring formal political conformity.

18. Ruedy, op. cit., p. 251.

19. L. Rummel, 'Privatization and Democratization in Algeria', in J. Entelis & P. Naylor, *State and Society in Algeria*, Boulder – USA: Westview Press, 1992.

20. H. Roberts 'The FLN, French Conceptions, Algerian Realities' in E.G.H. Joffé (ed.), *North Africa: Nation, State and Region*, London: Routledge, 1993, pp. 111-142.

21. E.G.H. Joffé (1995), 'Algeria: the Failure of Dialogue', in S. Chapman (ed.), *The Middle East and North Africa*, London: Europa Publications, 1995, p. 8.

22. H. Roberts 'Algeria Between Eradicators and Conciliators', op. cit.

23. This was enshrined in the January 1995 St Egidio Accord signed between the FIS and seven other political formations in Algeria which required negotiations as a first step towards ending the violence. The regime's official position has been that violence should end first, to be followed by negotiations.

CHAPTER V

SUFI BROTHERHOODS IN CONTEMPORARY ALGERIA

Sossie Andezian

The dominant form of North-African Sufism has traditionally been marked by a strong devotion to holy personages, shaykhs, friends of God (*awlīyā'*, sing. *walī*) the closest equivalents within Islam to the 'saints' of Christendom. This form of Sufism, rich in charismatic and ecstatic phenomena, has favoured the spiritual predominance not just of these shaykhs – legitimized or not by orthodox Islam – but also of a whole variety of people known for their devotion: wonder-workers, local patrons, heroes, even apparently 'foolish' men, deliberately incurring the blame of the mediocre, while inwardly possessed of some mark of grace, in virtue of which they command a mysterious respect, if not veneration. Those saintly personages are designated by the term 'marabouts' in French, referring to the Arabic word, *murābiṭ*.[1] Combined with social and political life, Sufism has given birth to saintly lineages and tribes which claim maraboutic descent. Later, some of these lineages and tribes will claim prophetic descent and will be recognized as *shurafā'* (sing. *sharīf*). This prophetic filiation is often fictitious but it is a means of legitimizing political power. Progressively, Sufi masters founded religious organizations, the *ṭuruq* (sing. *ṭarīqa*) or 'spiritual ways' translated by French administrators and scholars by the term 'ordres religieux' or 'confréries'. North-African Sufism is, then, a polymorphous and a polysemic phenomenon which played a great part in spreading and in rooting Islam in the area, as well as in fighting invaders, such as the Portugese, the Spanish, the Ottomans, and the French. It has contributed to the shaping of North-African identity right up to the beginning of the twentieth century, where it was challenged and supplanted by nationalist and reformist movements. New independent states continued this struggle against the brotherhoods, in their effort to modernize society and to purify Islam from what they considered as non-Islamic beliefs and practices.

Is there any place for Sufism in the Algerian religious field today, where Islam is a political factor engaged by different social forces? Despite being supposedly eliminated in the middle of the century by the reformist movement *(Iṣlāḥ)*,[2] Sufism still has its followers after Independence, but these are less numerous and less organized than in earlier centuries. Since the beginning of the 1980s, Sufism is said to have 'resurfaced' or 're-emerged'. As far as my own research indicates, Sufism has simply become more obvious, after many years of life underground.

In this chapter, I propose to analyse the contemporary roles and functions performed by Sufism in the area of Tlemcen located in western Algeria. The city of Tlemcen is known to have long been a place where different Islamic trends have coexisted. My purpose is not to lay stress on the permanence of traditional religious expressions but to emphasize the role of individuals and groups in shaping religious life in spite the prevailing policy of the state. The data I will discuss were collected by myself in the context of an anthropological study between 1981 and 1990. My insertion within the social networks of Sufi devotees was necessary to observe their practices and to collect the discourses concerning their practices and representations. This method allowed me to participate in the daily life as well as in the ritual life of a great number of persons and groups. The interviews were conducted in Arabic (Algerian idiom) or in French. Collecting data was an easy task, for the Sufi devotees were very proud to talk to a foreigner about their culture. I lived in the city of Tlemcen but I chose to take as an observational anchorage a family affiliated to the ʿĪsāwiyya brotherhood in Aïn el-Hout, a village located at the outskirts of Tlemcen, about ten kilometers from the centre. From this point, I could reach many other devotees, either members of the same brotherhood or of other brotherhoods. I could also reach Sufi devotees who were no longer members of any brotherhood. As a woman, I was usually present within female networks, but as a foreigner, I could attend some of the men's meetings and take part in their discussions. I was invited to many Sufi ceremonies as an outsider, but one who was nonetheless interested in Islamic spirituality.

In the 1980s, the practice of Sufism, such as I observed it in the city of Tlemcen and its surroundings (small towns and villages) is common, amongst women and men, amongst old and young, amongst rural and urban populations, amongst learned and illiterate people. It is characterized by devotion to the *awlīyā'*, whom devotees solicit as intercessors close to God. The communication with the *awlīyā'* is set up through special prayers, by visiting, and organizing pilgrimages to, their shrines. It is established as well by visiting their descendants (usually spiritual rather than hereditary ones) who take care of their shrines and transmit their doctrines to their followers. Sufism is practised either individually or collectively. Collective practice is organized within groups attached to brotherhoods.

The existence of a brotherhood involves an institutional framework: a *zāwiya* (sacred territory), a leader (of saintly descent), and groups (*firqāt*, sing. *firqa*) of affiliated members (*fuqarā'*, sing. *faqīr*). In the area of Tlemcen, this is the case for some brotherhoods: the ʿĪsāwiyya, whose *zāwiya* is located in the village of Oulhaça since the eighteenth century and the Ṭayyibiyya, whose *zāwiya* is located in the village of Nedroma. The two *zāwiyāt* constitute the western Algerian branches of Moroccan brotherhoods. The shaykhs of both brotherhoods are biological descendants of the founders of their *zāwiyāt*. They live there with their families which help them in their various tasks. Other brotherhoods, such as the ʿAlawiyya, founded in Mostaganem in Algeria, the Darqāwiyya, founded in Morocco, the Algerian branch of the Qādiriyya founded in Mascara, the Shīkhiyya founded in el-Bayyad in Algeria, have no main *zāwīyā* in Tlemcen but one or two secondary ones. There is no shaykh living there; only a delegate of the shaykh (a *muqaddam,* fem. *muqaddama)* takes care of the *zāwīya* and receives the *fuqarā'.*

Endowed with the *baraka* (blessing) of the founder since his birth and designated as the head of the brotherhood because of his rank in the family (usually he is the eldest), a shaykh must nevertheless possess personal charisma in order to gain the full confidence of the devotees. His task as a religious leader consists in receiving visitors who come to venerate their spiritual ancestors or seek *baraka.*

The shaykh of the *Ṭayyibīyya,* Shaykh Abderrahman is known for his skill in healing sciatica and other neuromuscular diseases by piercing the auricula with a filament of brass. Like his brothers and cousins, he has inherited this skill from his grand-father, who acquired it in China. He works as a healer in the *zāwīya* and receives patients every day, whether they be affiliated to his brotherhood or not. He is assisted by a *muqaddam* who welcomes the patients and asks them some questions about the purpose of their visit. When the shaykh receives a patient, he starts the consultation with a long interview during which he asks precise questions about the symptoms, the circumstances when the pains appear, the kind of medical treatment already used. If he considers that the state of a patient necessitates conventional treatment, he counsels him to go to hospital or to consult such and such a physician. Otherwise, if he is sure that the patient is suffering from sciatica, he puts a buckle of brass filament in his auricula. Then he says some prayers invoking God's help through the chain of his ancestors. The patient gives him some money, according to his own discretion, for there is no fixed fee. The whole process is considered as a visit to the founder's shrine, a *zīyāra,* and the money given for the help received, as an offering to the founder. For the patients, Shaykh Abderrahman is only an intermediary between the patients and God, and his skill is a divine favour.

As to the *shaykh* of the *'Isāwīyya,* Shaykh Abdelkrim, he is able, like the founder of the *ṭarīqa,* to neutralize the bites of snakes and scorpions by sucking the wound. But he is seldom solicited for this skill. The *fuqarā'* visit him punctually when they need moral support. They talk to him as they would to a deeply trusted confidant about a wide range of problems: they speak of family conflicts (between spouses, between in-laws, between brothers and sisters, between parents and children); they ask his advice about the doctors they have consulted, as well as prayers in order to endure illness; psychological and spiritual problems are also raised. The shaykh, who seems to know each *faqīr* intimately, listens to them with great attention and solicitude. He gives everybody Qur'ānic inscriptions as *baraka*. He comforts and reassures them, urging them to place their trust in God's hands. Visitors may ask for his mediation between them and some public authorities, in the case of juridical matters for instance. As he knows the local authorities of his village, he can solicit them as intercessors. In return, visitors bring food and give him some money. They can stay at the *zāwīya* as long as they wish, for the *zāwīya* is said to be the house of the *fuqarā'*.

The working of a *zāwīya* depends largely on the activities of the *fuqarā'*. These are organized into groups or *firqāt* around a *zāwīya* located in their village or in their quarter of the city. In Tlemcen there are many *firqāt* attached to the different brotherhoods mentioned above, but each one functions differently. The *firqāt* of the *'Isāwīyya* brotherhood are the most numerous (about ten). All are headed by a *muqaddam*, a person named by the shaykh, enjoying the consent of the majority of the members, and who functions as both spiritual leader and practical manager at the same time. Usually, each group is divided into two sub-groups, male and female, the latter being headed by a woman, a *muqaddama*. The *muqaddam* and the *muqaddama* who represent the shaykh could be of saintly descent, but this is not a necessary qualification. The qualities needed for such a role are piety, good reputation, exemplary morality. To be educated is not essential: but the ability to memorize prayers is indispensable. And last but not least, a *muqaddam* and a *muqaddama* must have great capacity in managing inter-personal relationships, for conflicts between members are not unusual: discord over the organization of ceremonies, over the practice of certain rituals and ceremonies, or disputes over personal matters - all such conflicts require sensitive and, at the same time, firm handling. The shaykh intervenes only in cases where a conflict causes members to oppose the *muqaddam* or *muqaddama*, and when the conflicts endanger the equilibrium of the group. This was the case after 1990, when some members of the *ʿĪsāwīyya* brotherhood, for instance, influenced by Islamist ideology, tried to forbid the performance of certain traditional ceremonies involving song and dance, deemed un-Islamic in their eyes.

The function of *muqaddam* is not remunerated. Even the prestige obtained by such a position is relative, for it is recognized only in a limited circle, that of the affiliated. Such a position, impermanent and revocable as it is, can be challenged at any time.

The members of a *firqa* belong to all ages. It is not easy to determine the number of those affiliated to each brotherhood. Women seem to be more numerous nowadays; but this is less because of some change of heart on their part than because of the fact that Sufi brotherhoods have become more private, and less public/institutional. Being an affiliate does not necessarily imply the formal attachment to a *firqa*. Usually, one is affiliated by birth, but the idea of divine election or of voluntary affiliation remains very strong. Young and old mention the role an adult has played in their initiation (generally a grand-father for boys and a grand-mother for girls), with whom they entertain close relationships. In whatever way they may have become affiliated, almost all the persons I have met talk about their initiation as a process of sudden conversion during a ceremony, as an event of great importance in their life. They say that they have been adopted by the founder of the brotherhood during a ceremony or after a dream or some misfortune. Translated by the idea of the transmission of a secret or of the *baraka* of the founder, the initiation entails spiritual and moral teaching, learning prayers, music, chants, and trance dances.

The 'trance behaviour', which is a part of the traditional system of expressing feelings in families associated with brotherhoods in the area of Tlemcen, is transmitted to the children as a form of body language. This process starts in early childhood where babies are dandled while their mothers repeat the word *'izhid'*: 'go into a trance'. Later, the imitation of persons in a trance, a favourite game of children encouraged by adults, will constitute the best way of learning. This is a 'prestigious imitation' as M. Mauss put it[3] when young people observe older ones, whom they trust and who exert authority on them, effectively performing actions which have succeeded in the past. Originally a simple biological process, imitation becomes in such a context a form of social conduct.

Each male and female *firqa* (if the latter exists) of a brotherhood gathers separately, on a Thursday night or Friday afternoon, to perform a ceremony commonly called a *ḥaḍra* during which special prayers are performed, some enter into various kinds of trance, and, afterwards, discussion of spiritual, moral, and practical matters takes place. The *ḥaḍra* is founded on a circular system of exchanges between devotees and a saint-founder: request *(ṭalab)*, favour *(ʿaṭāʾ)*, visitation *(zīyāra)*, in other words, there is an exchange of speech, material goods and spiritual goods, a ritual sequence the most significant elements of which are constituted by purification, prayers, offerings, and sacrifices. Another set of exchanges, between devotees this time -an exchange of words, advice, mutual help, sharing of food – enhances the overall practical efficacy of the gathering which is thus at once ritual and social, symbolic and concrete, an expression of shared ideals and a participation in lived realities. Being pure in both body and spirit is absolutely necessary. The latter is alluded to by the word *nīyya* (intention), which is also the criterion of the sincerity of the *faqīr* towards God and the saint-founder, to whose authority he has submitted.

The *ḥaḍra* includes a sequence of Sufi prayers called *'dhikr'* (lit. 'remembrance/invocation) which consists in repeating liturgical formulas: Qurʾānic verses *(aḥzāb*, sing. *ḥizb)*, eulogies of the Prophet, pieces of poetry and chants composed by the saint-founder. The formulas vary from one brotherhood to another but in each one, the *ḥaḍra* starts with the recitation of the *Fātiḥa,* the first *Sūra* (Chapter) of the Qurʾān. The *Fātiḥa* is said before every ritual ceremony in Algeria in order to place it under the protection of God. The *Shahāda*, or the

Profession of Islamic faith, is another litany recited in this kind of assembly. The prayer of *dhikr*, which is the core of the *ḥaḍra*, begins with the repetition of the Names of God, particularly the Name *Allāh*, and ends with the repetition of the last sound '*h*' after having progressively eliminated the first two syllables of the Name. During the *dhikr*, devotees often go into a trance, the aim of which is existential communication with God, mediated through a relationship with the saint-founder, other major saints, or the Prophet himself. In some brotherhoods, such as the *ʿĪsāwiyya*, the *Qādīriyya*, the *Ṭayyibiyya*, there can be a musical accompaniment and trance-dances. The others (*ʿAlawiyya*, *Darqāwiyya*, *Tījāniyya*) produce trance states only by reciting litanies and chanting. The *ʿĪsāwiyya* devotees practice a set of rituals named *laʿab* or 'play' composed of dances with swords, knives and fire. Some of them swallow snakes, scorpions and glass, without any apparent harm to themselves. Only men practise the *laʿab*. They explain their ability to perform these feats without being hurt, by their love for God which annihilates all their physical senses and causes them to utterly forget their self, the aim of every Sufi.[4]

Besides the prayers, there is another set of gestures and acts the purpose of which is to facilitate communication with the saint-founder of a *zāwiya*: turning around his tomb, touching the cloth covering it, lighting candles, burning incense, sleeping one or several nights near the tomb, in the hope that the saint will appear in a dream, giving inspiration, advice or benediction. Sharing food (generally couscous prepared with the meat of sacrified animals) is desirable in *ḥaḍra*, but compulsory during pilgrimages, as well as when a person has been clearly blessed by the saint in some way. Named *baraka*, such food is mystically endowed with the qualities of the saint.

In all the *firqāt*, attending the regular meetings is not compulsory. Members come there if they have no other obligations. Their number grows during important celebrations. Usually in these circumstances, all the local groups come together. Information concerning ceremonies circulate through different networks: those of kinship, neighbourhood, friendship, and profession. Money is offered to the *muqaddam* of each group. Some of it is used for travels if necessary and the remainder is given to the shaykh. Apart from the meetings, affiliates seldom visit each other; but assistance is immediately forthcoming in the event of emergency or some extraordinary personal or familial event.

Ordinarily, each *firqa* functions as an autonomous network, but the bonds that tie many of its members to the members of other *firqāt*, such as friendship, kinship, or matrimonial alliance, ensure interaction with the other local *firqāt*. Otherwise, when a *firqa* is invited to perform a ceremony in family homes or in public places, it calls up all the other *firqāt* in order 'to make the performance succeed'. Then, many of them meet almost regularly and are in touch with each other.

The different local *firqāt* interact when they come together for the great annual event which is the pilgrimage to the tomb of the founder of the brotherhood. Each brotherhood has its own pilgrimage. Some one thousand people attend the ceremonies held during three days and more. Men and women stay in separate houses, even if they are married. Ceremonies performed by men are public, and women can attend them; while ceremonies performed by women are private, and men cannot attend them. Staying in the same place for many hours or days, sharing the same emotions, practising the same rituals – all of this tends to minimize the differences between the members of the brotherhoods who declare themselves to be spiritual brothers and sisters. The pilgrimage is an occasion for each shaykh to strengthen his position as leader by, for example: homogenizing the various networks; legitimizing the changes adopted by some networks (for instance modern musical arrangements of the chants by young people for the *ʿĪsāwiyya*); welcoming guests belonging to other branches of the brotherhood; or renewing ties with individual members of his own group.

HOW DO THE DEVOTEES EXPLAIN THEIR ATTACHMENT TO SUFISM?

I had many discussions with male and female devotees of the *ʿAlawiyya*, the *Darqāwiyya*, the *ʿĪsāwiyya*, the *Qādiriyya*, the *Shīkhiyya*, the *Ṭayyibiyya* and the *Tijāniyya*, either individually or collectively. On the other hand, I interviewed the shaykhs of the ʿ*Alawīyya*, the ʿ*Īsāwīyya* and the *Ṭayyibīyya* as well as at least one *muqaddam* and one *muqaddama* of all the brotherhoods mentioned. The main results can be summarized in what follows.

Belonging to a brotherhood confers upon its members a social identity even if it is asserted within the restricted networks of the brotherhood. The affiliation to a brotherhood entails a moral oblig-ation to participate in a system of exchange which is set up with hierarchical superiors, on the one hand, and with spiritual brothers, on the other hand. Each brotherhood proposes a set of values where love and fraternity have a central place.

If the five daily canonical prayers of *ṣalāt* embody and express obedience to the divine law, the *dhikr* and the trance are considered as means for expressing divine love, the supreme aim of every formal religious practice. The fervour and the enthusiasm which accompany the *dhikr* and the trance evince an intensity of devotion that far surpasses that which is found in the canonical prayers – the legal minimum of worship – demanded by the reformists. Although motivated by the desire of communicating with spiritual beings, the participation in a *ḥaḍra* initially implies contact with living beings (representatives of the saint, other devotees, other human beings). The relationship with the beyond seems to materialize through social relationship; the immaterial and the spiritual appear to take on form and structure insofar as the gatherings are dominated by a hierarchy of social rules, accepted and interiorized by the participants as an inherent part of the moral and spiritual discipline that must accompany effective communication with the beyond.

The relationship between the affiliates with the shaykhs is very close and is designated by the terminology of kinship. The shaykhs call the devotees 'sons' and the devotees call them 'fathers'. The devotees designate each other as 'brothers' and 'sisters'. The position of the shaykhs on the initiatic chain places them above the devotees and their 'perfection' in the Way makes them exemplary models to imitate, like the ancestors. The word *shaykh* means 'master' as well as 'old, aged' in the sense of a wise man, whatever his age. The proximity between a shaykh and his affiliate is expressed by gestures of hospitality. One cannot go out of a *zāwīya* without having eaten at least a piece of bread as *baraka*. In the *zāwīya*, the affiliates – and ordinary visitors – always find a corner to take a rest, to sleep, to spend one or several nights.

The ultimate social function of the shaykhs is to negotiate the position of men in modern societies by reducing the distance between two ethics, two worldviews, two ways of behaving. Mediators between earth and heaven, body and spirit, between men and women, between individuals and social groups, the shaykhs become, in times of politically important change, mediators between past and present. In the religious sphere, they 'negotiate' a relationship between affiliates and God, in the institutionalized framework of beliefs and practices they 'negotiate' the position of Sufism in the sphere of political and religious power. They specify their own role in comparison with the official imams by redefining their rights and duties towards God and men, the spiritual Hereafter and the social herebelow. They outline again the frontiers between the sacred and the secular.

The shaykhs deliberately dissociate themselves from the economic sphere even if devotees pay them for *baraka*. The counterpart of that marginality is a greater autonomy. But their activity is not subversive for, rather than putting themselves forward as rival power holders, the shaykhs stand firm with the common people. The power they possess, attributed to their spiritual charisma, is considered as a 'clean' power, used for good purposes.

Nevertheless, the efficacy of the shaykhs is not always guaranteed. Their authority is threatened by the instability of their social position and can be challenged at any time: they are then forced to prove continually their efficacy with authoritative, laudable, and sensible actions.

NEW SOCIO-POLITICAL CONTEXT AND THE REORGANIZATION OF THE BROTHERHOODS

When I was back in Algeria in 1990, five years after my last fieldwork in Tlemcen, many changes had occurred within the brotherhoods, chief amongst which was the fact that they were much better organized and endowed with a higher degree of overall legitimacy. It is important to explain this significant evolution in the form and status of the brotherhoods.

The changes observed in 1990 must be placed in a historical perspective. The position of the brotherhoods was greatly weakened after Independence; but this situation began to change in the beginning of the 1980s, that is, the period after Boumedienne, when a marked improvement gradually made itself felt. Some of the *zāwīyāt* which were rather deserted were again frequented; old branches were reconstituted, new ones inaugurated; young boys and girls joined the brotherhoods to which their parents or their grand-parents were affiliated; ties were forged between regional branches of the same brotherhood that had either had no previous relationship or had allowed old ties to lapse (this is the case for the *'Īsāwīyya*, for example). Brotherhoods like the *Tijānīyya*, suspected of collaboration with the colonial authorities or those, like the *'Alawīyya*, considered as politically dangerous in the view of the newly independent state, were rehabilitated, for they were seen to have been successful in spreading Islam, in Africa for the former and in Europe for the latter (Islam was introduced in parts of Africa in the nineteenth century through the *Tijānīyya* brotherhood; as to the *'Alawīyya*, it has converted and still converts a siginificant number of Europeans to Islam). Political scientists have explained the modification of the position of the Sufi brotherhoods as the effect of their manipulation by the state in order to counter-balance the fundamentalist movement. But the process by which the brotherhoods have re-emerged in Algerian society is more complex, being the effect of the conjunction of many factors. The years referred to were marked by attempts at rehabilitation of local and regional cultural specificities (ethnic, linguistic, religious), that were covered up after Independence, in order to construct a unified nation-state and to define a homogeneous national identity. These attempts at local re-affirmation led to the democratic process which began in 1988 but which was halted by the current acute socio-political crisis. Despite the crisis, the right of association allowed informal brotherhood networks to organize more formally. Also, very significantly, the government gave back the *zāwīyāt* or the lands of the *zāwīyāt* it had appropriated during the Agrarian Revolution. The greater visibility of the brotherhoods was also related to the religious policy of the government which let so-called independent imams[5] administer religious life. This semi-liberal policy gave rise to new religious leaders among whom there were Islamist imams as well as shaykhs of Sufi brotherhoods. The development of the Islamist movement helped to reveal a diversity of religious currents in Algerian society, hitherto hidden behind a veil of religious uniformity, upheld for the sake of an ideologically motivated image. The re-emergence of the brotherhoods was thus favoured by the new socio-political context. They were even encouraged by the government to organize themselves. For instance, in 1991, the 'Association of the Zaouias' was created, in order to restore the spiritual heritage of Algerian culture.

If the Algerian Sufi brotherhoods were able to reorganize themselves so quickly, it was because many of them were previously functioning as informal social networks, at a local or regional level. The brotherhoods of today are restructured from these networks. Also it must be stressed that brotherhoods are not reorganized from the top, but from below. And if the pressures exerted by some fundamentalist militants in order to convert the leaders as well as the members of Sufi brotherhoods to their ideology has succeeded in some cases, in many other cases those members resisted strongly and claimed the full legitimacy of their beliefs and practices. Besides the usual supporters of Sufism, many intellectuals who had fought against Sufi brotherhoods after Independence, subsequently praised them for their role in safeguarding Algerian historical identity. And last but not least, if Sufism is still important in Algeria now, it is principally because individuals and social groups have continued faithfully with the practice of that religious form despite the fluctuating policy of the government towards it. One can therefore assert that Sufism constitutes a key element of the Algerian psyche, living on both in the collective memory and in current practice; it can thus be mobilized as a source of identity at all times, and especially during periods of political and social crisis, when questions of identity, legitimacy and morality are brought sharply to the fore.〜

NOTES

1. *Murābiṭ:* literally, one who is attached to a *ribāṭ*, a military and religious 'convent' were Sufis used to live or to gather in the middle ages.

2. *Iṣlāḥ:* literally, reform or amelioration. This refers to the movement attached to the *Salafiyya* which is a political, social, cultural, and religious reformation movement which spread all over the Muslim world during the beginning of the century. As implemented by the Algerian *'ulamā'*, *Iṣlāḥ* tended to redefine Islam with reference to its primary sources: Qur'ān, Ḥadīth and Sunna (Tradition of the Prophet) and to reorganize private and social life in conformity with Islamic norms and values. Organized into an association in 1931, 'The Association of the Algerian Muslim *'Ulamā''*, the *'ulamā'* fought Sufi brotherhoods accusing them of encouraging ignorance and backwardness within the Algerian nation.

3. In his *Essais de Sociologie*, Paris : Minuit, 1969.

4. S. Andezian: 'La confrérie des *Isāwa* : de la transe rituelle en Algérie.' *De l'émotion en religion: renouveaux et traditions.* F. Champion and Hervieu-Léger (eds). Paris : CNRS, 1992, pp. 505-532.

5. Independent imams are religious leaders who are not civil servants.

CHAPTER VI

THE BERBER ISSUE IN ALGERIA

Brahim S. Nali

Unless you know where you are coming from,
you wouldn't know who you are.
And unless you know who you are,
you wouldn't know where you are going.

Issues relating to Berber culture and identity and to the Berberist
movement, although having a long history in the Algerian
context, have been pushed to the forefront of political debate by
the events in Algeria in recent years. A close look at these events
indicates that the Berber question continues to play a central role in
them and remains an extremely important factor affecting future
developments in this country. In order to understand the implications
of this debate for Algerian society, it is necessary to set a framework
wherein these questions can be properly addressed. The Berber issue
has not just emerged out of nothingness nor has it evolved in
isolation. It has a history and a dialectic. Above all, it has come to
represent the expression of a people who find themselves at a cross-
roads in their history.

WHAT IS THE BERBER ISSUE? WHAT IS BERBERISM?

There is no doubt that what comes to mind when we talk of the
Berber issue are the demands that Berbers formulated for the preservation of their language and culture. These purely cultural demands

constitute the kernel around which Berberism was first moulded into a movement. However, the Berberist movement has undergone a profound evolution and today its course is being altered by two new factors. First, a 'political' element emerged within the movement (as opposed to the original 'culturalist' one). As a result, the Berber cause has been overshadowed by side-issues and reduced to a mere battle-ground where ideological conflicts are pitched. The second factor is the emergence of an 'extremist' group. Ideas of federalism and separatism began to circulate and old myths and fallacies pertaining to Berber origins and alluding to a Christian past began resurfacing. These issues can only be properly debated within a socio-historical framework.

We will begin this chapter by presenting some ethnological and demographical data about the Berber people. Their history from ancient times to the modern period will then be reviewed emphazising the differences between the successive phases and highlighting the role played by the Berber element in each of them. This review, descriptive in its account, covers all the sections except the last one. Its aim is to give the socio-historical background of the Berber issue and to contribute thereby to the ideas being debated within Berberism. In the last section (the descriptive and normative account), we look at Berberism and, while placing it in its historical context, we address the problems it is facing at the present time. Essentially, we will argue:

1) that 'political' Berberism is detrimental to the interests of the Berber cause;

2) that Berber cultural rights are best served when framed within a 'Human Rights' approach.

We will also propose a number of points which we believe should advance the Berber cause.

THE BERBERS

Addressing the Berber issue inevitably begs the question: Who are the Berbers? Very little is known about them in comparison with other peoples. There is no doubt that it is as a result of Ibn Khaldun's work that the Berbers were recognized as a separate people. His monumental work, the *History of the Berbers*[1] became the principal source of information for historians and anthropologists of the Maghreb. Still, most of the work in this field in modern times has been authored by French scholars. The above question is far from being trivial. To address it properly we will consider two elements common to all the Berber groups: the land they occupy and the language they speak.

Geographically, the Berbers are all inhabitants of North Africa where they are distributed in groups over large expanses of land. (To get an idea of the areas involved, consider that Algeria alone is the size of the whole of western Europe). Ample evidence exists to indicate beyond any doubt that they have been in these lands well before the Roman and Punic periods and as such they are rightly recognized to be the indigenous inhabitants of North Africa.[2]

In present day North Africa, Berbers can be found living in eight countries: Algeria, Morocco, Tunisia, Libya, Mali, Niger, Mauritania, and Egypt. Generally, they live in towns and villages, except for the desert nomads, and form a number of groups, subgroups, clans and tribes. Probably, an important factor that has contributed to the emergence of so many groups is the varied geography of the inhabited space and the changes in the climatic conditions from one area to another within this space. An example of this is readily available in Algeria. There, we find Berbers in the mountainous region of Kabylia overlooking the Mediterranean sea (*Kabyles*) and in the narrow plains along the coast (*Shilha*). They are also found in the highlands and in the desert. In the Sahara, they live in the Aures mountains region (*Shawiya*), in towns (*Mzabs* in Ghardaia) and the southern part of the desert in the Tassili n'Ajjer region (*Tuaregs*). The climate in the region as a whole has also undergone dramatic changes in the course of millennia since prehistoric times. All this diversity has had a dual effect on Berber culture and society: while being a source of enrichment it also had at times a negative influence affecting their unity and cohesiveness.

For Berbers, language is probably the most distinctive trait. Their name is derived from their language as Ibn Khaldun explains: 'Their language is foreign and different from all others: this is why they are called Berbers [...] In Arabic, the word *berbera* means a mix of unintelligible sounds.'3

In fact, Berbers never call themselves by this name. They are more likely to use specific tribal names (as in *Yeghomracen*) or the group name (as in *Lak'vail* or Kabyles). To designate the larger family of Berbers, they would use *Imazighen* (singular: *Amazigh*) and a derivative of this word, *Thamazighth*, to indicate their common language. All these words derive from the same root *Mazigh*, the common ancestor of all Berbers.4 For them, the word *Amazigh* designates a 'free' or 'noble' man. The various dialects make up the ensemble that we call the Berber language. Ethnologists classify Berber in the Afro-Asiatic family of languages and distinguish five large Berber subgroups (Eastern, Northern, *Tamasheq*, *Zenaga* and *Guanche*). The Kabyle language, for instance, belongs to the Northern group. In all, these groups subdivide into 33 forms of language.

Accurate demographical data about Berbers are not easily available but an estimate of 15 to 20 million, inclusive of all the countries and the large immigrant communities in Europe and elsewhere, is not unreasonable.5 Of these, there are around 5 million Algerian Berbers, with the *Kabyles* and the *Shawiya* being the largest groups and about 10 million of Moroccan origin with the *Shilha* and *Drawa* tribes representing the dominant Berber groups.

Across thousands of years, Berbers have kept a bond not only through a common linguistic heritage but more importantly through a distinctive culture that has survived till the present day. It is this Berber culture that essentially defines the Berber people. However, capturing and describing such an elusive (yet so omnipresent and all-pervading) element is certainly more difficult than accounting for Berber lands and languages. Ibn Khaldun, who lived amongst them under their own dynastic rulers, gives a meticulous account of their history and sums up his description as follows:

> We believe we have presented a series of facts that prove that the
> Berbers have always been a powerful, fearless, brave and numerous

people; a true race like so many other races in this world such as the Arabs, the Persians, the Greeks and the Romans.[6]

North African prehistory is at best sketchy and the meagre archeological data that exists is generally a subject of debate, and prone to controversy and conflicting interpretations.[7] What is clear, however, is that around 30,000 years ago, this region was already settled by Homo-Sapiens and that a Capsian stone industry was present around 7000 BC in the area. At around this time, dramatic changes in the climate started taking place and as a result plant and animal life flourished in the hitherto desert areas, and hunting and cattle herding became the principal activity of these tribes. From this age, lasting for over 4000 years, many archeological sites have survived in the form of dolmens, cave engravings and pottery work, giving us a glimpse of life in these early settlements. It seems reasonable to posit that the new climatic conditions in the Sahara must have eased communications between the peoples of the region stretching from the Nile to the Tassili region in southern Algeria. As the Sahara region dried out again, the former tribal activities became gradually replaced by sedenterization and agriculture. This latter may not have been developed locally but it is very likely that it came to the region as a result of the contact with the Egyptians. Furthermore, these contacts must have also stimulated cultural and political developments so that by the end of the second millennium we see evidence in the Central and Eastern regions of the emergence of a state, at least in an embryonic form.

Already at the time of Ibn Khaldun, the question of Berber origins was being debated. The issue was raised again during the French colonial period in an attempt to surmise that Berbers were of European origin.[8] This theory is not sustainable nowadays; the consensus seems to be that the inhabitants of the region have probably come from a variety of groups, some hailing from the East and some indigenous to the region.[9]

THE PUNIC AND ROMAN PERIODS

The first contacts of the Berbers with the Phoenicians were

probably on a very small scale spanning a long period during which they traded with Phoenician sailors who gradually established small settlements along the coast. The founding of Carthage in 814 BC by the Phoenicians followed a treaty with the local chiefs and this indicates to us that Berber states at this time had already evolved some rudimentary structure. The coexistence of the two societies was peaceful and had some effect on Berber society, helping its structure to develop further. As Carthaginian influence spread along the coastal areas, the Berber states grew in strength in the interior regions. The first 'Numidic' Berber kingdoms (as the Carthaginians called them) date back to this epoch. This period of peaceful coexistence lasted for over six centuries until it was brought to an abrupt end by the Roman attack on Carthage and the ensuing Punic wars (264 - 146 BC).

In the course of these wars, the Berber king, Massinissa, took the initiative to consolidate his rule, founding Cirta (modern Constantine) as his capital and expanding his kingdom. With the end of the Punic wars, the victorious Romans turned their attention to the Berber kingdoms then ruled by Jugurtha, the grandson of Massinissa. In defence of his kingdom, Jugurtha faced up to the Romans, waging against them a relentless war (the Jugurthine war, 112-105 BC).

The destruction and slaughter inflicted on the Berbers during this war became marked in their collective memory, and from that time the land of the Berbers knew only insurrections and popular revolts. Their legendary bravery, rebelliousness, and stubbornness that Ibn Khaldun describes at such length, probably stuck with them since these times. The Romans were effectively ruling the country either directly or through the local aristocracy who levied taxes and sent agricultural produce to Rome. Hoping to quell the rebellions, they introduced a policy of coopting the Berbers and Romanizing them. This also failed, as the Berbers relentlessly pursued their rebellions and guerrilla warfare. The best known Berber rebel leader (and still a hero for present day Berbers) from this period, Tacfarinas, started a general revolt (17-24) that engulfed North Africa and reached the confines of Mauritania.[10]

When the Vandals invaded some coastal towns in 429, they were not met by any Berber resistance. The Berbers still considered the Romans to be the real enemy and this new invasion offered them the opportunity to escape the direct control of Rome. Berbers rediscovered a new taste for freedom and self-rule so that when the Byzantines reconquered the lands from the Vandals, they were faced by an even fiercer resistance. As Berbers continued to destroy the symbols of the former Roman hegemony, the Byzantines abandoned their attempts to collect taxes and barricaded themselves in the cities. The rule of the Byzantines itself was to be short-lived, as a few decades later the Arabs defeated them in North Africa, heralding a new phase of outside intervention in Berber history.

The religion of the Berbers throughout this time is also highly indicative of the collective response of Berber society to the different encounters. Archeological evidence from shrines and other sites indicates that the Berbers had several gods in antiquity. It also shows that, during the Punic period, they shared some beliefs with the Phoenicians, while there is no evidence that they were influenced by the religion of the Romans in the pre-Christian era.

In the period preceding Christianity, Berbers were also exposed to Judaism and a number of tribes converted to this religion, so that when Christianity reached North Africa, Berbers had already become very familiar with monotheism. From the beginning, Christianity was identified with the Romans and as such was the religion of the invaders. It took a long time for the new religion to gain followers and when it did, it was mostly in the urban areas, amongst the aristocracy and the coopted Berbers.[11] There is little evidence that it made any significant impact in the countryside. In consequence, when the Muslims arrived at the region, they found a number of tribes still practising Judaism,[12]and others sticking to their age-old pagan beliefs, an indication of how little Christianity had taken root there. Ibn Khaldun tells of one such Judaic tribe lead by al-Kahina at the time of the Muslim encounter:

> Some of the Berbers followed Judaism, a religion they adopted [...]
> The Djeraoua tribe which inhabited the Aures and to which Al-Kahina
> belonged, was one of these Jewish tribes.[13]

THE MUSLIM PERIOD

The next era in the Maghreb starts with yet another people arriving, this time from Arabia. The new religion, Islam, started in Mecca in the year 610. By the year 640, Egypt was under Muslim rule, followed by Tripoli two years later; and in 647, the first expedition was sent from Egypt to Byzacenia (Maghreb). Four or five expeditions later, the Maghreb became part of the Muslim world and by the year 709 an army composed of Berbers and Arabs headed by the Berber Tariq Ibn Ziyad, was preparing to cross into Spain through the strait that would eventually bear his name.

By all accounts, this was an extraordinarily successful campaign, and it is little wonder that some speak of paradoxes when confronted with these facts.

1) In all some four or five expeditions were sent.

2) In the first one, the Byzantines were defeated (their king Gregory was killed in battle).

3) Some Berber tribes converted to Islam.

4) Other tribes presented fierce resistance. Among these, notably, was the resistance of al-Kahina which resulted in the killing of the leader, Hassan bin Nuaman and the resistance of Koceila, leading to the killing of Okba Ibn Nafi.

5) During the last expedition, agreements were reached between Musa bin Nusayr and the Berber chiefs, securing an end to the revolts and paving the way for mass conversions and voluntary enrolment in the army. The substance of these agreements is not known but it seems that Musa bin Nusayr succeeded in convincing the Berber chiefs that the Muslims were primarily interested in the propagation of Islam and not in the usurpation of Berber lands.

The 8th century was marked by a number of revolts, especially in Morocco and Spain. Not much is known about this period but it appears that the revolts arose as a result of the reintroduction of direct taxation or as a consequence of the political wrangling taking place in the East.[14] The Khārijites' movement developed among the Berbers as an expression of their rejection of the orthodox version of Islam and opposition to the style of rule and administration. A number of small states emerged for short periods, but by the end of the century, the whole of the Maghreb seemed to attain a high degree of stability and, more importantly, a quasi-autonomous status vis-à-vis the caliphate in the East. From this moment onwards, we see the newly Islamized Berbers playing a full part not only in the political struggles but also in the religious divisions between the Maghreb and the Orient. This is clearly borne out by the succession of dynasties that ruled the Maghreb until the beginning of the 13th century: Aghlabids, Idrissids, Fatimids, Zirids, and Hammamids. As argued by Laroui,[15] this period corresponds to the time when the Maghreb was in the process of defining its identity. Berbers participated fully in all these dynasties, revolts and historical processes and, most of the time, led them. Successively, they tried out a number of ideologies which reflected their full involvement in the religious debate, and, in the process, strengthened their autonomy and independence. Khārijism, Zaydism, Shīʿism were all tried out until orthodox Malikism finally triumphed under the Al-Moravids and became firmly rooted in the lands of the Maghreb.

By the year 1060, the new dynamic group, the Al-Moravids, emerged in the Maghreb. Buoyed by their mission of bringing Muslims back to an orthodox Mālikī Sunnī Islam, under their Berber leader Yusuf Ibn Tashfin, they managed to unite the small states. Under the inspiration of another Berber leader, Ibn Tumart, the Almohads ('the unifiers') completed the work of their predecessors and brought the whole Maghreb under one rule. Although it did not disintegrate completely, their rule as a unified dynasty was nevertheless short-lived and soon, the 'unifiers' themselves became segmented into three Berber states. This period was followed by an age of decay marked by a series of wars and internal squabbling. Ibn Khaldun (1332-1406) lived during this period traveling throughout a decaying empire and, inspired by his experiences and observations, he developed his cyclic theory of history. Later on, the Turks intervened to resist the continuous European and particularly Spanish intrusions and in the process swallowed the Maghreb into the Ottoman Empire.[16]

THE COLONIAL PERIOD

With the French invasion of Algeria (June 14th, 1830) there began a new cycle of violence and conquest that was to have far reaching implications for all Algerians. At the time of the invasion, Algerian society was far from being vibrant; it was still in the state of stasis and decay that Ibn Khaldun had so meticulously described. Yet, this conquest turned out to be very much like the thousand-year long Roman attempt at absorbing Numedia and ended up very much in similar fashion.

No sooner had the French set foot on Algerian soil than rallying cries for resistance were reverberating throughout Algeria. The Emir Abdelkader in the west of the country and Ahmed Bey in the east lead the early resistance. By 1847, and the end of this early phase of resistance, the French had still to subdue the Kabyle region: it took the building of a 'Fort National' amidst the rugged mountains and years of ferocious fighting to suppress this insurrection. There was hardly a single year without some rebellion breaking out in some part of the country. The legendary figures of the Kabyle leader al-Mokrani, of the Kabyle woman Lalla Fathma n'Soumer and the resistance of the Ouled Sidi Cheikh in the South come to us from this period. In 1871, the whole of Kabylia erupted under the leadership of al-Mokrani and the *Rahmānīyya* Berber Sufi brotherhood. The warfare spread out, rapidly engulfing other regions in Algeria and reaching the Aures and Bousaada in the south. Then, gradually, the uprisings started to diminish and lose their intensity, so that by the end of the century most of the country seemed subdued and resigned to its defeat.

However, around the turn of the century, political movements with the common aim of freedom began to form. These movements expressed their ideas mainly through three groups: the revolutionaries, under Messali Hadj, who advocated the overthrow of colonialism by force; the Muslim *'Ulamā'* headed by Sheikh Ben Bādīs, who sought national awakening through religious reform; and the liberals, headed by Ferhat Abbas who favoured the gradual introduction of social and political reforms to safeguard Algerian rights. In the face of French intransigence, none of these movements was able to bring the dream of independence any closer to fulfilment so that, by the beginning of the 1950s, some leaders began to realize that armed struggle was the only alternative. In November 1954, war was declared against the French and eight years later (in July 1962), Algeria came to its new existence as an independent nation.

Just as in the early years of occupation, the Berber regions and leaders played a key role in the political movements and armed struggle leading to independence, so Berbers were also strongly present in the *Association of Muslim 'Ulamā'* as well as in the other nationalist movements. Though Messali Hadj, Ferhat Abbas, and Ahmed Ben Bella are not Berbers, their close associates, Lahouel Hocine, Ahmed Boumendjel and Hocine Ait Ahmed respectively were all Kabyles. In all formations, Berbers could be found in key positions, and at no point was there any serious thought of forming an ethnically based party. The only exception to this was during the so-called Berberist crisis of 1949, when Kabyles in France voiced their opposition to Messali Hadj's definition of the Algerian people as an Arab nation.[17]

Following the dismantlement of Messali Hadj's movement by the French police, the only revolutionary organization that continued to operate in 1949-54 was the new clandestine group headed by the Kabyle leaders Krim Belkacem and Amar Ouamrane in Kabylia and Mustapha Ben Boulaid in the Aures mountains. At the launch of the war, these two groups formed the backbone of the resistance. Right from the beginning of the war, Berbers were strongly represented in the leadership committees both inside Algeria and abroad. From the Soummam Congress in 1956 until the end of the war, their contribution to the leadership fluctuated between 20 and 45.[18] This high level of representation in the leadership, proportionately much higher than their representation in the Algerian population at large, was a reflection of the contribution of the Berber regions to the war effort.

Throughout the colonial period, French policy towards the Berbers was based on the 'divide and rule' strategy. This aimed at isolating the Kabyles from their Arab neighbours, a strategy that was clearly expressed by the opening of a large number of schools and the intensification of missionary work in Kabylia. At the same time, the 'academic' departments launched their 'discovery of the Berbers'.[19] Research articles, reviews, and extensive studies under the authorship of 'eminent' historians, ethnologists, and a variety of other field specialists were devoted to the task of proving that the Berber people shared a common origin with the Europeans. An example of these is Edouard Bremond's book[20] entitled: 'Berbers and Arabs: Barbaria is a European country'. This colossal academic enterprise was geared towards 'helping' the Berbers 'rediscover' their origins and their Latino-Christian heritage, thus freeing them from the shackles and backwardness in which the Arabo-Islamic culture had supposedly trapped them. In Morocco, this approach was even more forcefully implemented with the creation of the so-called 'national Berber park'. None of these attempts worked, as all Algerians clearly knew who was their real enemy. This does not mean that individuals were not aware of their ethnic identity. Nor does it mean that they had just put aside their enmity temporarily in the face of a common enemy. It is simply that, although tribes had a strong sense of ethnic identity, they felt bound to one another through Islam and this super-seded any ethnic considerations. The following extract from a letter of Ben Bādīs back in 1936 illustrates this (author's translation):

> The sons of *Ya'rub* (the Arabs) and the sons of *Mazigh* (the Berbers) have been united by Islam for more than ten centuries. And throughout these centuries, they have never ceased to be closely united with one another in bad times and good times, so that from ancient times they constitute one Algerian Muslim element whose mother is Algeria and whose father is Islam. [...] After all this, what force is capable of coming between them? [...] They never did disunite when they were powerful, how could they now that others are holding power? By God, no! And all attempts to divide them will only serve to reinforce their unity and consolidate their bonds.[21]

To summarize this historical section of the chapter: The history of the Berbers is a story of encounters on two levels: one being the level of people and the other, that of ideas and cultures. The two aspects are intimately intertwined, with the cultural encounter reflecting the nature of the encounter between the peoples. The following is a schematic overview of these relations.

a) Carthaginian: Peaceful coexistence. Berber states emerge.

Berbers adopt some Punic deities.

Some Berber tribes convert to Judaism.

b) Roman: State of war and resistance.

No evidence of any religious influence.

c) Christian Roman: Continued resistance.

Some Berbers convert to Christianity mostly in urban centres.

Berber Christians follow the Donatist church which rebels against the Roman church. Most Berber tribes keep their pagan or Judaic beliefs.

d) Muslim: Resistance in the first years.

Less than 100 years later, most Berbers are Muslims.

Berbers rule a succession of states and dynasties, autonomous and independent.

e) French: Continued resistance.

Failure of cooption policy.

Failure of missionary work.

This indicates that Berber relations with other peoples fall within two categories which can be defined according to the manner in which the Berber social psyche perceives the encounter:

1) Peaceful encounter: Characterized by open-mindedness to new ideas, resulting in cultural and religious exchanges.

2) Invasion or foreign domination: Marked by sustained resistance and a minimum of cultural or religious influence.

Berbers have experienced both types of encounters, the first with the Carthaginians and Muslims, and the second with the Romans and the French.

THE POST-INDEPENDENCE PERIOD

Although the Ben Bella period was highly unstable because of internal power struggles, these disputes did not spring from divisions along ethnic lines. Berbers, and more specifically Kabyles, could be found in all camps and disagreements were as much between them as they were between opposing groups. Power and ideology were stronger cohesive factors affecting their allegiances than was the ethnicity of the individual. Even the armed insurrection in Kabylia in 1963 led by Ait-Ahmed was not ethnically motivated.[22] Berberism was rarely an issue in the ruling class and in the political elite. It is thus not surprising to find that there is a consensus among political scientists with regard to this point:

> Conflicts within the Algerian political elite have been both
> frequent and intense but with rare exceptions they have not revolved
> around issues of regionalism, separatism or ethnicity.[23]

However, the first catalysts of popular Berber discontent were appearing in this early period. As the power struggles were taking place, Berber public opinion interpreted them as acts of discrimination aimed at keeping their war heroes away from the seat of power. These feelings were further exacerbated by the realization that, despite the fact that Kabylia bore more than its fare share of the brunt of the war, its leaders continued to be marginalized and exiled. Berbers still held some important positions in the new *nomenklatura*, but this was considered to be a direct consequence of their generally superior education enabling them to operate as technocrats within the bureaucracy. Real power, however, was not in their hands.

During the Boumediènne period, Berber representation in the leadership was at a record low but the government, being very much conscious of the potential ethnic problems, worked to counterbalance this fact by heavily investing in the Berber regions, in areas such as education, infrastructure, and industrial development. However, the government also embarked on an Arabization programme, the negative effects of which were soon apparent. This programme was started on a small scale just after independence but was now relaunched on a larger scale, swept along by the influence of Arab nationalists. Although never officially stated, Berberism, and more specifically Kabyle Berberism, came to be viewed as a major obstacle on the road to a total Arabization of Algeria.

Up to that point in time, Kabyles had not felt threatened by Arabic, the language of their religion. The launch of the Arabization campaign, however, made them feel that they were being targeted and some started to regard Arabization as a process detrimental to their culture. This was probably unexpected on the part of the government but not so much for observers such as Quandt who, back in 1972, asked:

> Under what circumstances might ethnic politics develop [...] ? A major impetus towards ethnic politics would be the adoption by the government of policies actively hostile to the Berber minority. These might include rapid Arabization, the neglect of economic development in rural Berber areas and the exclusion of Berbers from political and administrative positions within the government.[24]

And that is precisely what happened.

BERBERISM AT A CROSSROADS

One event stands out in Berber collective memory as a symbol of a direct and unveiled attempt at the de-Berberization of Algeria: the directives to limit the broadcasting time of the sole Berber radio channel in Algeria. This decision affected primarily the ordinary Kabyles, especially women and inhabitants of remote villages, who tuned regularly to this station for Berber music and culture. People voiced their resentment pointing out that even French fared much better in the Algerian media. Under threat, Berbers started rallying around their common cause. Berberism was born as an opposition to what was regarded as an Arab nationalist regime.

The activities of this movement went generally unnoticed by Algerian society until the events that led to what became known as 'The Berber Spring'. On April 19-20th 1980, triggered by a cancellation of Mouloud Mammeri's lecture on Berber poetry, a wave of demonstrations by students in Tizi-Ouzou soon spread in the region, culminating in riots in the town and on university campuses. This undoubtedly marked the dawn of Berberism. The ideals of this movement were concretized in that year during the Yakouren meeting around the following ideal: 'The recognition and defence of the Berber language and culture'.[25]

Reinvigorated by new blood and spurred on by the relative easing of restrictions on cultural activities, the movement embarked on an extremely dynamic phase in the 1980s, focusing on the recording of aspects of Berber life and culture: oral traditions were collected, poems transcribed, linguistic studies and translations intensified, and short essays and novels published. The launch of academic journals, *Tafsut* and *Awal*, further highlighted the dynamism of this period. Non-academic activity was also boosted by the dissemination of old Kabyle terminology and the growth of Berber folk and popular music, mainly through the work of musicians such as Lounis Ait-Menguellet.

If the dawn of Berberism was in 1980, the dawn of Democracy arrived in October 1988 when popular riots in Algiers spread to other regions and ended in the massacre of hundreds of civilians. Following these events, the government announced reforms that would, it was hoped, pave the way for a multi-party system. A plethora of parties was formed and registered to contest the local elections of June 1990. Quandt, considering the emergence of just such conditions, specu-lated on the consequences for Berberism:

> A second means by which ethnic politics might grow in impor-tance in Algeria could come, ironically, through the liberalization of the political system.[26]

Figures from the past, such as the Kabyle war hero Hocine Ait-Ahmed, returned from exile and entered the political race relaunching his old party FFS (*Front des Forces Socialistes*). The Berber movement, spurred by the liberalization process, either organized itself within the RCD (*Rassemblement pour la Culture et la Democratie*) under the leadership of Said Saadi or joined the ranks of the FFS.

The 1990 local elections and the December 1991 general elections saw overwhelming support for the main Islamist party, FIS (*Front Islamique du Salut*), with the then ruling party FLN (*Front de Liberation National*) being relegated to second place. In particular, the 1991 elections pointed out the weak representations of the FFS and RCD (combined number of votes of 5.36%) in comparison with the FLN (12.17%) or FIS (24.59%).[27] The regional distribution of the votes showed another interesting feature of these results: whereas the votes of the FIS and FLN covered all the different provinces, the FFS and RCD votes were largely confined to provinces in Kabylia. It is unlikely that this situation would change even if Kabylia were to join forces with other Berber regions. Above all, the limited performance of the FFS and RCD indicated the nature of the problem the Berberist movement was facing in electoral terms. Only 20%, at most, of Algerians are Berbers and it is thus inconceivable that any existing or future parties identified with Berberism could one day be successful on a national scale. This was just a reflection of a much deeper problem that touches the essence of the Berberist movement.

This fact hit the movement hard, which, having departed from the doctrinal text of Salem Chaker and Said Saadi – 'The Berber cultural movement is not a political movement: it does not develop any global political program that would define a precise political alternative. It is the open gathering of Algerians who cannot recognize themselves in the official definition of national identity...',[28] – now realized that going 'political' does not necessarily equate with success.

Hence the dilemma: to remain within the boundaries of this definition or to turn the movement into a political platform. As Chaker points out, two poles have emerged within the movement: the 'culturalists' and the 'politicals'. The former continued their work mainly in the cultural associations while the latter organized themselves within the FFS and RCD. As a consequence, what used to be a diversity has turned into a confusion over the essence, means, and aims of the movement. As a result, ideas advocating a federalist framework for the country (and even more extreme ones orbiting around separatism) have begun to circulate.[29] This represented the emergence of a distinct group with its own agenda based on these extremist ideas.

Even from the Berberist point of view, events were not evolving smoothly; the need to reassess the situation became urgent. Salem Chaker courageously presents some elements of the problem and discusses some alternatives, but in the end he fails to identify any solid option along what he termed the narrow road (*'la voie étroite'*). As we will argue here, widening this *'voie étroite'* would entail a number of factors which take into consideration the ethnological profile of Algeria as well as the socio-historical background in which the Berbers have evolved. These factors are discussed below.

1) BERBERISM AND ETHNICITY

First of all, it seems essential that the fallacy and myth of an existing distinction between Berbers and Arabs in Algeria should be addressed. Although it is true that Berbers did not mix and inter-marry with other peoples on an extensive scale, it is also true that they did so to some extent with friendly peoples. The campaign for Berber culture should not be accompanied by the myth of the 'pure Berber'. On the contrary, the Berber cause has much more to gain by focusing the attention of all Algerians on their common Berbero-Arab roots. Anti-Arabism cannot be the proper response to the hegemony of Arab Nationalism.

2) CULTURAL VS. POLITICAL BERBERISM

The dilemma arising from the 'cultural' versus 'political' bipolarity within Berberism should be resolved. The Berber movement is a cultural movement and any other form of Berberism such as the 'political' one amounts to a hijacking of the Berber cause and its subjugation to the ideological interests and political ambitions of an individual or a party. This is even true among Berberists: '...there is often on the part of Berber politicians an opportunistic instrumentalization of their social base.'[30] Cultural Berberism is not an ideology, but merely the expression of a movement to work towards the defence and preservation of 'Berberness' (the state and identity of being Berber) and the dissemination of Berberophony with its vehicular language.

3) BERBERISM AND PARTY POLITICS

The corollary of the above point is the need to dissociate the Berber movement from party politics. Any close identification of Berberism with a particular party or politician will generally bear negative results as illustrated by the following examples. Consider the rapprochement between the RCD's leader and the government as cited by Chaker: '... Its founder [the RCD's] has readily confirmed that he is disposed to participate in a presidential majority',[31] and its negative impact upon Algerians. Another example relates to the staged kidnapping of the Kabyle singer M. Lounes that resulted not only in so many broils amongst Berbers but more importantly in discrediting the Berber cause.[32] Such associations inevitably make the Berber cause a hostage in the hands of a group and subject it to the vagaries of party politics where power does change hands and sympathies do fluctuate. The Berber cause should not be condemned to such an uncertain future and to remaining a pawn in the hands of politicians.

4) BERBERISM AND IDEOLOGIES

The Berber cause should be kept outside the ideological battle-ground. At the moment, it is clearly being drawn into some camps which have their own ideological motivation for being anti-Muslim or anti-Arab. How are we to understand the failure of the Berberist movement to secure the support of all Kabyles? This phenomenon, highly paradoxical at first, can only be explained with reference to the fact that the Berbers, who are mostly Muslims, having perceived anti-Muslim elements within this movement, withheld their support. In general, such elements within the Berberist movement, being antago-nistic towards either Islam or the Arabs, are tarnishing its image and limiting its appeal to a wider electorate. Berberists will have to decide whether to clean up their ranks or let these 'ideologues' use the Berber cause to further their aims at the expense of the wider Berber cause. Furthermore, Islam is not and cannot be inimical to the Berber cause with its cultural aspirations. In my opinion, it protects 'Berberness' (*la Berberité*) and supports Berberophony. Not only does it not conflict with cultural Berberism, the essence of the Berber movement in its early phase, but it positively backs its demands. As for political Berberism, it all depends on its underlying ideology; and more often than not, this hidden ideology will clash with Islam.

The place of Berbers within Algerian party-politics and ideologies is another factor needing careful attention. To Chaker's statement that 'there are as many visions [within the Berberist movement] as there are Berberists', one should add: *'There are as many Berber positions as there are parties and ideologies'*. This is an inescapable reality. It is a plain fact which the Berberist movement has failed dismally to take into account. Berbers have been active players within all tendencies before, during, and after the War of Independence. Today, their ideologies also range over a wide spectrum including the FLN, FIS, the PRA, and others. Some of the key leaders in these parties are Berbers. The exclusive association of the Berber cause with a party such as the RCD is tantamount to limiting its scope. Of course, each Berber has an ideology and a belief system; it is the latter that should be put at the service of the Berber cause and not the reverse.

CONCLUSION

Throughout their rich and eventful history, the Berber people of the Maghreb have been through many encounters. Confronted with new ideas from friendly nations, their open-mindedness enabled them to benefit from these ideas, while their resilience and rejection of foreign domination helped them to withstand the challenges and thwart many absorption plans. Their culture today, still rich and vibrant, speaks to us down the ages having triumphed over many hegemonies and survived the vicissitudes of history.

In modern Algeria, the Berberist movement started as a cultural movement challenging the hegemony of Arab nationalism. Today, it is facing a new and greater challenge and dilemma: whether to remain true to its original ideals or to become political. For many Berberists, this latter option seems inevitable and at the moment it is winning the debate. However, as discussed in this article, this option is fraught with danger as it will undoubtedly alienate a large section of the Algerian population and polarize it along ethnic and political lines. It is thus detrimental to the true Berber cause and, as has been argued above, will only serve the ambitions of some political parties and foreign masters.

The logical consequence of the arguments developed in this

chapter is that the Berber cultural demands should be elevated to the status of 'human rights', challenging all parties and groups to support them. This, however, will only be possible if the Berberist movement returns to its origins, distances itself from politics, and finally clears its ranks of 'ideological' elements. The resulting movement will undoubtedly advance the interests of this cause much further.

Just like in Roman times, the cooption of some Berber elements is doomed to failure and, true to its history and nature, the Berber people will again find its own path and voice. There are more serious challenges ahead which will hopefully lead to the building of a just and mature society in Algeria.〜

NOTES

1. Ibn Khaldun, *Histoire des Berbères et des dynasties musulmanes de l'Afrique Septentrionale*, Trans. Le Baron de Slane, Paris: P. Casanova, 1925.

2. See C.-A. Julien, *Histoire de l'Afrique blanche des origines à 1945*, Paris, 1966, pp. 17ff; and G. Camps, *Aux origines de la Berbérie: Monuments et rites funéraires protohistoriques*, Paris, 1962, pp. 14ff.

3. Ibn Khaldun, op. cit., p. 168.

4. Ibid., p. 184.

5. *The Ethnologue*, 12th Edition, B.F. Grimes Ed., Dallas, Texas: Summer Institute of Linguistics, 1992.

6. Ibn Khaldun, op. cit., p. 199.

7. See G. Camps, *Aux origines de la Berbérie*, op. cit., pp. 14ff; and G. Camps, *Les civilisations préhistoriques de l'Afrique du Nord et du Sahara*, Paris, 1974.

8. A. Laroui, *The History of the Maghreb*, Princeton, 1977, p. 20.

9. Julien, op. cit., pp. 17ff.

10. Laroui, op. cit., p. 31.

11. Ibid., p. 50.

12. Ibn Khaldun, op. cit., p. 208.

13. Ibid., p. 208.

14. Laroui, op. cit., pp. 90ff.

15. Ibid., p. 126ff.

16. Ibid., p. 248ff.

17. W. B. Quandt, 'The Berbers in the Algerian Political Elite', in *Arabs and Berbers*, E. Gellner & Micaud (Eds.), London, 1972, p. 289.

18. Ibid., p. 300.

19. Laroui, op. cit., pp. 20, 342.

20. E. Bremond, *Berbères et Arabes: la Berbérie est un pays européen*, Paris, 1950.

21. A. Merad, 'Le Réformisme Musulman Algérien', PhD Thesis, Paris, 1967, p. 20.

22. Quandt, op. cit., p. 294.

23. Ibid., p. 302.

24. Ibid., p. 303.

25. S. Chaker, 'La voie étroite: la revendication Berbère entre culture et politique', *Annuaire de l'Afrique du Nord*, Vol.28, (1989), pp. 281-296.

26. Quandt, op. cit., p. 303.

27. M.S. Tahi, 'The Arduous Democratization Process in Algeria', *Journal of African Studies*, Vol.30, No.3, (1992), pp. 397-419.

28. S. Chaker and S. Saadi, *Tafsut: Etudes et Debats*, V1, 1983, p. 150.

29. Chaker, 'La voie étroite ...', op. cit.

30. Ibid.

31. Ibid., and *Le Monde*, 5th October 1989, p 6.

32. See *La Tribune* 31st May, 1996, *L'Express* 3rd June, 1996.

CHAPTER VII

THE CULTURAL AND ARTISTIC
HERITAGE OF ALGERIA

Michèle Messaoudi

T he soil of the area known today as Algeria bears the remains of a rich and varied historical past: Phoenicians, Romans, Vandals, Arabs, and Ottomans have all contributed to a cultural patrimony which is largely dominated by Berber, Arab, and Ottoman influences that fertilized the region in the spiritual ambience of Islamic civilization, and which has been eroded by 130 years of French colonization. A mere overview of this legacy that does not touch on the problems of culture in contemporary Algeria would hardly do justice to a subject that is central to the development of the country. The postcolonial efforts of re-construction and development have failed to a large extent because the successive governments have overlooked some essential factors of culture.

Christianized in the 2nd and 3rd centuries A.D., the region fell to the Vandals in the 5th century, was recaptured by Byzantium in the 6th century and conquered by the Arabs in 681-682. Muslim rule was first exercised by the Abbassids, then by the Shī'ite Fatimids who were overthrown in the 11th century by a Berber dynasty, the puritanical Almoravids, themselves to be deposed by a more puritanical Berber dynasty, the Almohads who ruled directly until the 13th century. It was under those two dynasties that the region was to experience the greatest intellectual and artistic development, in close connection with that of Muslim Spain. The succeeding dynasty, the Abdelwadids, ruled central Maghreb from the 13th to the 16th centuries, initially on behalf of the Almohads of Morocco; although this dynasty had to cope with constant internal unrest – Tlemcen was taken from them by the Merinids from Morocco from 1337 to 1347 and from 1352 to 1359 – they managed nonetheless to contribute to the typically Maghrebi style of architecture. Tlemcen became capital of the region in the 14th century but fell to the Ottomans in 1550. The Ottoman empire brought enough stability to the region to allow the renewal of a flourishing culture but, in its decline, could not resist the assault of European colonialism. When France invaded Algeria in 1830, 130 years of ruthless colonial rule had begun, characterized by a policy of political apartheid and systematic de-culturation.

Leaving aside a few prehistoric and Roman remains, the first signs of a culture that helped shape the contemporary Algerian landscape go back to the Almoravids and Almohads who affirmed the renewal of Sunni Islam by developing a style of architecture that was a clear expression of their religious doctrine. From the Islamic point of view, architecture is the art form *par excellence* because of its social and spiritual function. It is therefore not surprising if the major component of the cultural heritage of Algeria is monumental.

The Great Mosque of Algiers (1097) and that of Tlemcen (c.1136), erected by the Almoravid Sultan Yusuf ibn Tashfin, were built in the same style as the Qarawiyin Mosque in Fez and other Maghrebi mosques, all built on the Andalusian model of the Cordoba mosque.

Several elements characterize the Maghrebi style of architecture. Champions of a strict orthodoxy and of a return to simplicity, the Almoravids were keen to express the austerity of their reform through the art form that has the greatest impact on the people, architecture. Under their leadership, and even more so under that of the Almohads who reproached them with indulgence and ostentation, a real artistic revolution took place, rejecting any sign of facile luxuriousness and promoting the blank space as a central feature of design to achieve harmony. It is the same use of empty spaces that contemporary architects find so appealing. The skilful mix of blank spaces and arches of various shapes and sizes, creating different volumes and a definite sense of harmony, also fills them with wonder.

The Almohads drew on the Medinan model in architecture as well as in *fiqh* and other matters. Their mosques carried on the tradition of the Prophet's Mosque in Medina with square minarets whose height is five times their width, and that of al-Aqsa Mosque with aisles perpendicular to the *qibla* to stress the orientation. From the outset, the prayer hall was wider than it was deep, in conformity with the way the worshippers lined up for prayer. The *qibla* was further emphasized by having from three to five cupolas enhancing its aisle, both inside and outside whereas the axial aisle never had any.

The highly decorative lobed arch that was developed in Spain was introduced into the Maghreb by the Almoravids. Here, it was given an even more spectacular treatment since the traditional five-lobed Andalusian arch was replaced with seven, nine, and eleven-lobed arches. As in Spain, a serpentine motif was widely adopted to remedy the weakness inherent to the lobed arch in its lower part, as can be seen in the Great Mosque of Tlemcen. By using, alongside the lobed arch, much simpler arches of different shapes, curvatures, and sizes in the same room, such as the prayer hall of the Great Mosque of Tlemcen, the architects managed the extraordinary feat of creating balance and harmony where one could have expected a baroque effect.

Another element of the Maghrebi style is the use of *muqarnas*, cellular honeycombs in stalactite form, exploited to great effect in Spain and the Maghreb where they first appeared at Tlemcen. The octagonal and ribbed cupola in front of the *miḥrāb* displays a very rich decoration of *muqarnas* which themselves became the ceiling. The making of the *muqarnas* depends on an art of brickwork that was developed in regions specializing in that material. The use of brickwork alternating with stone, especially in arches, is also typical of Andalusian and Maghrebi art. The Great Mosque of Algiers was entirely built in brick.

The only part of the mosque the Almoravids and Almohads allowed themselves to decorate lavishly was the *miḥrāb*, symbol of the invisible presence of the Prophet. That of Tlemcen is particularly striking with its cupola as described above, sitting on lobed pendentives, and its beautiful stucco panels with inscriptions and floral motifs in relief. Another characteristic of Maghrebi architecture is the use of palms, acanthus leaves, and pine cones in relief work. The inscriptions are in the highly ornemental *kūfī* style.

Apart from the Great Mosque of Tlemcen, known as the jewel of Algerian Maghrebi style, the following are also worth mentioning: the mosque of Nedromah, as simple as the Great Mosque of Algiers; the Abdelwadid minaret of Mansourah, the only remaining part of the mosque of this fortified place near Tlemcen; the Merinid mosque and *medersa* of Sidi Bou Madyan, practically the only examples of sumptuous stucco decoration in Algerian architecture.

Older buildings testify to the local taste for absolute simplicity, human proportions, and symbiosis with nature. The pillars of Sidi Okba mosque, near Biskra, were made of palm trunks, like the first mosque built by the Prophet himself. In the south, the building material is *toub*, a mixture of dried earth and straw, renowned for its marvellous insulation properties and now rediscovered by contemporary architects. The latter agree that their greatest lesson in architecture is given them by the people of the M'Zab, a Kharijite community who seceded from Muslim orthodoxy soon after the Prophet's death. Often labelled as 'the Puritans of the desert', the M'Zabites developed an architecture totally devoid of decoration, focused on design, function, and structure that expresses the human will to concentrate on what is essential and not to stray into vain distractions.

The other main influence in Algerian architecture is the Turkish one. Most of the mosques of Algiers, Annaba, and Constantine, the Casbah – the Turkish city – and numerous buildings of various functions – baths, schools, etc., – date back to the Ottoman empire. The main features of a Turkish mosque are the square hall covered with a cupola sitting on pendentives, the introduction of decorative tiles, and the use of marble for pillars. The French destroyed a large number of Turkish buildings and considerably altered some mosques so as to use them as churches and cathedrals.

In calligraphy, the quintessential art of Islam, the region has developed a distinctive Maghrebi script, which seems to have been flourishing around 1000. It is a cross between the angular *kūfī* and the rounded *naskhī*. It has the distinguishing feature of exaggerated loop extensions below the lines of the final forms of certain letters. The system of diacritical marks used in the Maghreb did not differ greatly from that used in the Mashreq. However, the proportioned system of writing devised by the Iraqi calligrapher Ibn Muqlah (d. 940) was never widely adopted in North Africa. What is now known as Maghrebi is an amalgamation of *Andalūsī*, characterized by finer lines, more compact form and considerable elongation of horizontal and under-line strokes, and *Fāsī*, larger, heavier, and more elaborate.

In the field of thought and literature, the region produced its share of mystics, poets, and theologians. Emir Abdelkader (c.1807-1883), the first leader of armed resistance against French colonization, is a moving example of a fine military leader who was also a poet, a thinker, and an author of spiritual works. The Turks re-introduced Andalusian poetry which gradually penetrated all levels of society. The *muwashshaḥ*, introduced into Spain by Ziryab in the 9th century, was composed in a language accessible to the masses, one which stood between literary Arabic and the local dialect. Simplified grammar and a rich vocabulary had produced a medium well suited to the popularization of a new culture, less scholarly and speculative, but more dynamic and lively. The *souk* was the colourful forum for the Turkish shadow theatre, the *qaraqouz* and for tales, legends, and epics to be told, mimed, or sung. Few names have reached posterity due to the oral nature of this tradition.

Closely connected to poetry is music, another popular art form. What is known as classical Algerian music is in fact Andalusian music, based mainly on the *muwashshaḥ*. Ziryab was a composer, poet, singer, and teacher at the Cordoba court who codified Andalusian music. The *nawba* – a complex suite of musical pieces expressing very different moods – of which twelve out of twenty four have been passed on to our time, is still played on special social occasions in the very form fixed by Ziryab, a miracle of jealously preserved oral tradition. The popular *r'arnata* are poems originating from Grenada, set to music. The contemporary *shaabi* is a popularized version of Andalusian pieces. The conservatories and orchestras of Constantine and Tlemcen have played a leading role in the preservation of the Andalusian heritage. There is a strong, living tradition of *madīḥ*, poems in praise of the Prophet, set to simple music and *nashīd* (hymns) of a religious or patriotic nature, most of which were written by the *ʿulamā'* of the Reformist movement in the 1940s and were first sung by the members of the scout organization they set up as part of their programme of cultural resistance.

Apart from this musical and literary legacy, the art forms that are still anchored in popular tradition are those referred to as crafts in Western terminology. From the Islamic point of view, there is no dictinction between art and crafts, the latter being as noble as the former. The enamelled silver jewels of Kabylia with their red coral insets and filigree decorations are a legacy of medieval times, transmitted through a chain going from Persia to Byzantium to Spain where the Muslims inherited techniques introduced by the Vandals, that survived due to their 'naturalization' in isolated, mountainous regions. It is the women who have perpetuated the century-old traditions of pottery – with red and brown decorations on a yellow background in Kabylia – basket work and weaving (rugs, cushions, blankets, clothes). The mats that cover the floor of simple dwellings as well as mosques are made with doum palm fibre on the weft, and esparto on the warp, woven on a high loom like rugs. The traditional carpets are made of wool, thick and characterized by geometrical designs woven in parallel bands on a brown, rust, dark red, or white (Sahara) field. Rugs from Kabylia incorporate letters of the Berber alphabet; those of the east display oriental influences brought in from Tunisia. Some Central Asian motifs have also been 'naturalized' since Ottoman times.

Sadly, the quality of workmanship has seriously declined to the point that some of the present offerings are mere shadows of their glorious ancestors. The avid commercialization of 'native' products in the 1920s, the 1929 economic crisis and the pressures of colonization have led to the production of much inferior items and the disappearance of some, such as fine leatherwork embroidered with gold or silver and fine embroideries in silk, gold and siver thread on tulle or silk. The surviving embroideries of gold and silver on black velvet are pale reflections of a formerly sophisticated art form.

The first French generals who invaded Algeria in 1830 remarked that there were comparatively more literate people – and more educated girls – in Algeria than in France. The colonial administration quickly implemented a comprehensive programme of de-culturation aiming at undermining the fundamental components of Algerian culture: the Arabic language and Islam. The religious and cultural resistance offered by the ʿUlamāʾ Association of Shaykh Ben Bādīs managed to preserve the most basic cultural elements such as Qurʾānic recitation and elementary *tafsīr*, Qurʾānic commentary.

Alienation from the national language, and therefore history, is central to the problems of culture in Algeria today. Acculturated by 130 years of colonization, Algerian artists and writers have been alienated from their Islamic roots to the point of feeling these roots to be 'religious constraints', and in their attempt to escape the suffocation of political dogma, they have sought and found a semblance of freedom, creativity, and originality in Western role models – ironically, but inevitably, mainly French.

Artists called for symbols of Berber, Arab, and Muslim culture, the three main components of Algerian culture, but lacked an accurate and complete knowledge of their own aesthetic history because they could only learn it through the distorted perception of the orientalists. In the case of calligraphy, which traditionally forms the basis and the essence of the artistic expression of *tawḥīd* (unity), most of the well-known artists have used Arabic letters as mere elements of design, devoid of linguistic meaning. In the wake of Mondrian, Matisse, Kandinsky, and Klee, Mohammed Khadda and Abdullah Benateur in the 1950s were the first Algerians to interpret Arabic calligraphy as 'pure abstraction'.

In the 1960s, artists of all media – painters, writers, film makers –

became the bards of the revolution and its socialist agenda. Apart from the recent past of the Algerian war of liberation and the achievements of the socialist regime, the theme that was at the forefront of literary works was that of national identity. Some writers poignantly expressed their dilemma: 'I think in Algerian and I write in French words that cannot express everything', wrote Boualam Khalfa in 1962. Malek Haddad aptly expressed the alienation of Francophone writers: 'I am not so much separated from my motherland by the Mediterranean sea as I am by the French language. Were I to write in Arabic then I would still be screened from my readers, by illiteracy ... I am incapable of telling in Arabic what I feel in Arabic ... The French language is my exile.' The intelligentsia is on the fringes of society, mistrusted by the people who cannot relate to totally westernized or hybrid art forms and who judge cultural activity as unimportant on the scale of social priorities.

The Algerian thinker Malek Bennabi (d.1973) addressed the problem of culture in a much deeper way. For him, cultural stagnation or regression underlies under-development in any society. Algeria was colonized because it had made itself colonizable after centuries of post-Almohadian fog that culminated in the numbing practices of maraboutism. Colonization provided the necessary stimulus to rouse it from its slumber. Its renaissance was initiated by the Reformist and Nationalist movements. Bennabi establishes a link between man's efficiency, the soil on which he lives, and the time in which he lives. Under-development results from the inefficiency of all the individuals in the society, of people who have not learnt how to use their primary tools, the soil, and time, or who have stopped learning how to do so. Schooling alone cannot solve the problem of culture but it can play a part if it fits within the framework of a wide cultural project. What makes a culture is a favourable environment. Bennabi also highlighted the place of women as the main propagators and preservers of culture and outlined the present limits to this vital role.

Culture must be part of a social contract: there must be reciprocity between society which demands a particular pattern of behaviour from the individuals and the individuals who demand a particular way of life. In a civilized society, both social constraint and the critical attitude of the individual are fundamental aspects of the social function of culture. This reciprocity can only be exercised if there is a social cement binding the individual to the social body. Bennabi explains that societies seem to have based their cultures on either ethical (Semitic people) or aesthetic (Aryan people) values. Soon after independence, he called for a synthesis of truth and beauty as a basis for Algerian culture, to be achieved in the shortest possible time.

The socialist regime did work on a cultural project but failed to motivate the people. Corruption, nepotism, the betrayal of the original Islamic character of the revolution, dictatorship, and censorship have de-motivated a people who paid a high price during eight years of bloody armed struggle. The problem of culture in Algeria remains that of giving a meaningful content to the essential activities of a people facing vital difficulties and not that of giving a content to the leisure of a minority. The proponents of the Islamic project think that an updated synthesis of Islamic ethics and aesthetics would provide the vital social cement for the development of a true culture in Algeria. The longer their project is foiled, the harder the task of re-motivating the whole nation will be and the more difficult it will be to convince people who have been deprived of the most basic necessities for so long that culture is more important than agriculture – to use one of Bennabi's images.◠◡

BIBLIOGRAPHY

Les grands thèmes, Malek Bennabi, Omar Benaissa ed., Algiers, 1976.

Les conditions de la renaissance, Malek Bennabi, written in 1948 but published by the students of the mosque of Algiers University in 1971.

The Cultural Atlas of Islam, Lois Lamya and Ismail R. al-Faruqi, Macmillan Publication Company, New York, 1986.

Islam and Muslim Art, Alexandre Papadopoulos, Harry N. Abrams Publishers, 1979.

Les mosquées en Algérie, collection "Art et culture", SNED, Algiers,

1974.

Tlemcen, collection "Art et culture", SNED, Algiers, 1974.

Les arts indigènes féminins en Algérie, Marguerite A. Bel, published by le Gouvernement général de l'Algérie, 1939.

Les bijoux de Grande Kabylie, Henriette Camps-Fabrer, collections du Musée du Bardo et du Centre de Recherches Anthropologiques, Préhistoriques et Ethnographiques, Algiers, 1970.

Contemporary Art from the Islamic World, edited by Wijdan Ali, Scorpion Publishers Limited, on behalf of the Royal Society of Fine Arts of Amman, London, 1989.

La littérature algérienne d'expression française, Ghani Merad, P.J. Oswald, Paris, 1976.

Les nouvelles tendances du roman algérien de langue française, Guy Daninos, ed. Naaman, Quebec, 1979.

Le cinéma algérien, Lotfi Maherzi, SNED, 1980.

FROM SUFISM TO TERRORISM:
THE DISTORTION OF ISLAM IN THE POLITICAL CULTURE OF ALGERIA

Reza Shah-Kazemi

When we think how few men of real religion there are, how small the number of defenders and champions of the truth – when one sees ignorant persons imagining that the principle of Islam is hardness, severity, extravagance and barabarity – it is time to repeat these words: 'Patience is comely; and God is the source of all succour.'

(The Emir ʿAbd al-Qādir al-Jazāʾirī[1])

The main aim of this essay is to point to the way in which Islam in the political culture[2] of Algeria has been reduced from its intrinsic nature as an all-encompassing religion to the status of a narrowly-conceived ideology, from a lived reality of faith comprising legal, moral, and social duties, to a contrived programme of external action dictated by the exigencies of power politics. The most extreme form of this reduction is the ugly spectacle of terrorism masquerading as *jihād*. Nothing could be further from the spirit of Islam than a political campaign involving the murder, maiming, and terrorizing of unarmed non-combatants; but before Islam could be used as a pretext for terrorism, it had first to be politicized; and before being politicized, it had first to be secularized or, what is tantamount to the same, desacralized. This spiritual decline involves many obvious factors connected with colonialism, urbanization, and modernization, which have been analysed in various works; but the aim here is to direct attention to some of the less obvious ways in which the spirit of Islam in the political culture of Algeria was progressively displaced, marginalized, and in some extreme cases even subverted, by the subtle forces of modernism and secularism.

On the one hand, the phenomenon of terrorism in the name of Islam has its roots in the desacralization and politicization to which the religion has been subjected over the past century and more; and on the other hand, it is a reaction to the policy of repression brutally implemented by the military-dominated Algerian regime since 1992. If one's aim is to understand the immediate political causes of the present appalling level of violence, then attention will be focused in the first instance on this repression of the state; but if one's concern is with the way in which Islam had become so reduced that it could furnish the ideological basis for extremist violence, then attention must be directed to the longer-term causes of the process by which religion had become all but divested of its spiritual substance. A double critique is thus needed: on the one hand, the phenomenon of terrorism must be categorically denounced in terms of uncompromising Islamic criteria; and on the other hand, the immediate responsibility for unleashing the present spiral of violence must be attributed to the military-dominated regime that annulled the 1991 elections and resorted to the most horrific repression of hitherto moderate 'Islamists'.3 While our concern here is with the religious side of the question, it is important to begin with a brief survey of the political scene that may serve as the background for our critique on the plane of religious principles.4

***

It might fairly be said that in Algeria today, there is not one but two forms of terrorism: the first perpetrated by the security forces, the second by the Islamists. For there can be no doubt that, since the annulment of the elections of 1991, a consistent element of state policy has been an attempt to uphold the *status quo* through the terrorizing of its Islamist opponents, the *Front Islamique du Salut* (FIS, Islamic Salvation Front), for whom an overwhelming majority of the population had expressed their electoral support. Not only was the party banned, but twenty thousand of its members and supporters – an overwhelming majority of whom were moderates, including large numbers of professionals, academics, journalists – were incarcerated in concentration camps in the Sahara in 1992.[5] It was this massively disproportionate and illegal response to the prospect of an Islamist government that propelled frustrated splinter groups into an armed uprising against the state.[6] There is no doubt that atrocities have been committed by members of the Algerian state security forces, and then attributed to Muslim groups in order to discredit them in the eyes of the public; neither is there any doubt that there are many *agents provocateurs* who have infiltrated the ranks of groups such as the *Groupe Islamique Armé* (GIA)[7], and then advocate and carry out terrorist acts; no one can deny either that torture, assassination, and concentration camps have become routine instruments of state policy.[8]

It has been widely reported, first by the state-controlled Algerian media, and then by the western media, that the Islamists are not only barbarous but also specifically anti-intellectual, citing their murder of journalists and writers known to be of a secularist bent. To put this point in proper political perspective, we can do no better than quote the following paragraph from François Burgat:

> Within the Algerian upheaval, many intellectuals were indeed assassinated … But when, in May 1994, Rashid Mimouni counted a dozen of them, their number was infinitely greater: there were several hundred of them, at the height of their career or fresh from university. They were caught unawares [by the state security forces] on the threshold of their houses, kidnapped in the middle of the night, tortured savagely and psychologically broken for life; or gunned down in the middle of the day in the presence of their families or in the loneliness of a prison cell – broken, stifled, electrocuted and, of course, buried away from any camera. Some of them were intellectuals like Rashid Mimouni or Rashid Boudjera [i.e., of a secularist orientation]. Others, in their hundreds – including the 1,224 teachers and lectures who were members or sympathisers of FIS arrested in 1992 – were intellectuals of a different persuasion [i.e., Islamists]… Yet

it was not until two years later that Amnesty's reports and a small number of journalists and academics – who decided to cut themselves off from the communiqués of the Algerian Ministry of Information – uncovered other sides of a reality which is much more ambivalent [than at first appeared].9

***

If it was necessary to give an immediate political context to Islamist violence – which, it should be noted, is still the domain of a minority of extremists, and is denounced by the mainstream FIS movement[10] – it is now important to make a criticism of this violence in terms of Islamic principles. For none of the above-noted factors of repression, however horrific, justifies the resort by Muslims to acts such as the assassination of unarmed civilians regarded as traitors because they had in some way collaborated with the regime. The ferocity of state repression may explain, but cannot condone, the practice of retaliatory terrorism. Many such acts have been committed by groups loosely affiliated under the name of the GIA, who claimed responsibilty for the murder of the thirty six Europeans, for example, killed in Algeria between 1992 and 1994.[11] The victims of such terrorism, or rather, of the civil war in which terrorism has become routine for both sides, now run into uncounted thousands. In a principial sense, the numbers involved are secondary: for even a single case of terrorist assassination is unjustifiable in Islam, however violent or despicable be the opponent. There are no mitigating circumstances that render excusable the perpetration of acts that violate the essential principles of the religion. It is not possible to establish Islam through means that denature Islam. The *Sharīʿah* forbids absolutely the murder of unarmed civilians – of this there can be no shadow of doubt. But it is not enough simply to repudiate terrorism in terms of the letter of Islamic law; one needs to go deeper and see how the very spirit of Islam had already been fundamentally misconceived for such acts to be even contemplated, let alone committed, in the name of the religion.

The extremists who have taken to terrorism would argue that one must 'fight fire with fire', that the descent into violence was the unavoidable consequence of the regime's brutal repression, that they had no choice but to resort to the only means of struggle left to them. Other, more moderate, Islamists will argue that, although such acts are indeed 'un-Islamic', criticism thereof should not outweigh condemnation of the regime, lest the overall legitimacy of the Islamist cause in its struggle against the tyrannical Algerian state be thereby damaged. Such a point of view, however, subordinates the integrity of Islamic principle to the logic of political expediency, and is thus to be avoided by all those for whom Islam is taken seriously as a religion, that is, as a source of values which, being of divine origin, infinitely surpasses the vagaries and vicissitudes of political life.

To highlight the error of both the extremist and apologist arguments in Islamic terms, one has only to recall the attitudes of the archetypal Muslim *mujāhid*, the Emir ʿAbd al-Qādir al-Jazāʾirī, who not only mounted the most successful resistance to the French between 1830 and 1847, but was one of the greatest Sufi masters in the Islamic tradition. At a time when the French were offering their soldiers a ten-franc reward for every pair of Arab ears produced, when severed Arab heads were regarded as trophies of war, and when whole Arab tribes were being slaughtered by the French, the Emir manifested his magnanimity, his adherence to Islamic principle, his refusal to stoop to the level of his 'civilized' adversaries, by issuing and forcing through, against much resistance from within his own ranks, the following unilateral edict:

> Every Arab who captures alive a French soldier will receive as reward eight douros … Every Arab who has in his possession a Frenchman is bound to treat him well and to conduct him to either the Khalifa or the Emir himself, as soon as possible. In cases where the prisoner complains of ill-treatment, the Arab will have no right to any reward.[12]

When asked what the reward was for a severed French head, the Emir replied: twenty five blows of the baton on the soles of the feet.[13] One might also cite, as an example of his fidelity to the spirit of the faith, his famous defence of the Christians of Damascus in 1860, where the Emir was living as an exile, having been defeated by the French. It is worth dwelling a little on this episode as it provides a salutary and much needed lesson for today's Muslims, in Algeria as elsewhere.

In the course of the civil war between the Druzes and the Christians in Lebanon, the Emir heard that there were signs of an attack by the Druzes on the Christians of Damascus. He wrote a letter to all the shaykhs of the Druzes, pleading with them not to 'make offensive movements against a place with the inhabitants of which you have never before been at enmity' – a clear sign of his sensitivity towards non-combatants. This proved to no avail, however, and a mob was soon approaching the Christian quarters; the Emir confronted them and urged them to observe the rules of religion and justice.

'What!' they shouted, 'you, the great slayer of Christians, are you come out to prevent us from slaying them in our turn? Away!'

'If I slew the Christians,' he shouted in reply, 'it was ever in accordance with our law – the Christians who had declared war against me, and were arrayed in arms against our faith.'[14]

This, too, had no effect, and in the end, the Emir and his followers sought out the terrified Christians and gave them refuge, first in his own home, and then in the citadel. It was estimated that no less than fifteen thousand Christians were saved by the Emir's actions, and in this number were included the European Consuls and Ambassadors. As his biographer Churchill prosaically puts it:

All the representatives of the Christian powers then residing in Damascus, without one single exception, had owed their lives to him. Strange and unparalleled destiny! An Arab had thrown his guardian aegis over the outraged majesty of Europe. A descendent of the Prophet had sheltered and protected the Spouse of Christ.[15]

One should note that this chivalric defence of the Christians extended even to the person of the French Consul: far from acting on the basis of resentment against the representatives of the forces that had defeated and exiled him, and that were still in the process of despoiling his homeland, he gave them sanctuary in his own home, thereby upholding the inalienable right of protection extended by Islam to all the 'People of the Book' that lived within the *Dār al-Islām*.[16] A greater contrast with the present self-styled warriors of Islam, so many of whom indiscriminately portray the West as the 'enemy' *tout court*, and perpetrate correspondingly illegitimate acts against westerners, could hardly be imagined.

How, one may reasonably ask, could Islam have become so corrupted in the period separating the great *mujāhid* from today's *Groupe Islamique Armé*? For it is not simply a case of comparing a 'good' Muslim to 'bad' ones; what separates the two attitudes is not just a difference of strategy or of tactics, but a mental chasm: they seem to belong to different spiritual universes. The question thus remains: how could the conception of religion have become so impoverished in the course of a century?

The immediate – and all too simplistic – answer given by Muslims is that French colonialism ruined Islam. While it is undeniable that Islamic institutions, practices, and even principles were indeed subjected to severe constraints and distortions, what is all too often overlooked is the degree to which Muslim responses to the secular influences of the French partook, unwittingly, in those same secular influences; and, in particular, how the campaign of the Salafis, in the name of 'reforming' religion, contributed significantly to the process by which religion was in fact divested of its spiritual substance, leaving it more akin to a social ideology with religious trappings, than a total world-view and way of life encompassing both spiritual and social dimensions.

While it would of course be wrong to draw a straight line connecting the Salafi reformists of the 1930s with the Muslim terrorists of the 1990s, it is nonetheless of the utmost importance, firstly, to take cognizance of the way in which religion was spiritually impoverished by the reformists, and secondly to note the relationship between this impoverishment generally and the phenomenon of politicized Islam, first within the state's ideological system and then, amongst extremists, as an inversion of this very system. One is not asserting that the Salafi influence was the main factor in the gradual desacralization of Islam, only that, of the several factors that are responsible for the impoverishment of the spiritual dimension of the faith, the negative consequences of the Salafi campaign are rarely taken into account. Indeed, the failure to note the extent to which Islam has been desacralized itself stems in large part from this very desacralization; attention is all too often directed towards the West as the cause of all Muslim woes, while the necessity of the spiritual regeneration of the faith is eclipsed by an all-consuming concern with the political re-assertion of Islam, conceived ideologically and territorially. It is hoped that the positive counterpart to an effective critique of Salafi influence in Algeria might be a re-evaluation of Sufism, not only historically, as a bastion of traditional Islam, but also in contemporary terms, as an effective antidote both to religious fanaticism and to modern secularism; for Sufism, as the repository of the wisdom of the Islamic tradition, can and should provide an ever-present means of establishing a just sense of proportions – that sense, precisely, which is woefully lacking in all those who imagine, to repeat the words of the Emir quoted at the outset, that Islam is 'hardness, severity, extravagance, and barbarity'.

***

'Islam is my religion, Arabic my language, Algeria my homeland', proclaimed the motto of Ben Bādīs, champion of the 'reformist' *'ulamā'*, to whom reference has been repeatedly made in the preceding chapters. Noone can doubt the importance of Ben Bādīs in defending native culture and in upholding certain Islamic values, the Arabic language, and elements of traditional identity; but, to quote Professor Bouamrane, the Algerians must have the courage to make an 'autocritique' on the question of the influence of the reformist school of thought associated with Ben Bādīs.[17] From the point of view of the spiritual decline of Islam that concerns us in this analysis, we would identify three main areas where such a critique seems warranted: the promotion of nationalism, the attack on Sufism, and, underlying both of these tendencies, an unconscious assimilation of modernism.

In promoting the idea of the Algerian 'nation' in the inter-war period, the reformists unwittingly downgraded Islam as the essential source of identity and orientation. The slogan cited above mentions Islam before the nation (*watan* being the Arabic word used), and thus formally gives primacy to religion over nationalism; that religion was indeed the mainspring of the attitudes and aspirations of the reformists cannot be doubted; and the idea of the 'nation' was promoted, at least in part, as a means to the attainment of religiously-conceived ends. Despite these sincere intentions, however, the very fact of incorporating such an alien, anti-traditional concept into the worldview of a new generation could not but have negative reper-cussions in psychological terms. For, once the idea of the 'nation', infused at is with the specific historical experience of Western Europe, entered into the thinking of this new generation, the integrity of the traditional mental ambience was greatly weakened. This was the first step in a slippery slope that led to the politicization of religion; for Islam was already being considered as a 'factor' in an equation that included an alien ideology, one that carried with it ramifications that could not be conveniently isolated and neutralized, still less 'Islamized'.

One notices a subtle inversion of priority: where traditionally, religion was the *raison d'être* of the 'people' – however defined – now, religion was one among other traditional elements that uphold the 'nation'. According to Ben Bādīs: 'It is in the safeguarding of our traditions (*taqālīdunā*) that lies the safeguarding of our national individuality (*qawmiyyatunā*).'[18] Islam was now an element of national identity; it was in terms of the 'nation' that religion became defined, whereas traditionally it was religion that defined the essence of individual identity. From this point of view, the Emir would be regarded as a true 'nationalist'; this is, at best, an ideological anachronism, and, more seriously, an insult to his religion, which transcends the narrowness implicit in nationalism. The Emir fought the French in the name of Islam, not in the name of the nation, which had neither a subjective reality in the minds of his followers nor an objective form in respect of institutional criteria.

It should be clear that this criticism of the reformists' attitude on the nation does not in any way imply support for the position of Ferhat Abbas, such as it was formulated in 1936 – the position that maintained that, since the Algerian nation 'did not exist', adoption of French nationality by the Algerians was the natural response. The Shaykh al-ʿAlawī, despite his reticence on political matters, nonetheless strongly discouraged his disciples from taking up French nationality, as this would involve losing Muslim personal status in legal terms; this same underlying resistance to assimilation was evinced by Shaykh Ahaddad who, as quoted in Chapter 2, fought against the French even while knowing that he would be defeated, in order to 'set a definite gap between our children and France, so that they would not mix with French children and become like them.'

In helping to generate nationalism as a focus of identity and orientation, the process of the secularization of Algerian society, already well under way, was significantly hastened; by giving religious sanction to a foreign, secular ideology, the way was paved for the more widespread insemination of a whole host of other ideas and forces emanating from the secular West: liberalism, socialism, and Marxism on the political plane; rationalism and scientism on the intellectual plane; and secularism, evolutionism, progressism, relativism on the social, psychological, and moral planes. The very act of defining one's identity in terms proper to an alien civilization and world-view effected a breach in the wall of traditional conceptions of identity, a breach through which these secular forces could make an entry and establish themselves more securely. What happened in Algerian society, especially after independence, proved the general principle that, once the focus is taken off religion as the exclusive and all-encompassing source of thought and orientation, the ideological positions unleashed by the segmenting power of individualism[19] are countless – whence the endemic conflict that has characterized the Algerian ruling classes since independence.

Returning briefly to the question of religious nationalism, it might be argued that the reformist *'ulamā'* felt that they had no choice but to 'prove' the existence of the Algerian 'nation', given the fact that the French not only denied this entity, but also, in a sense, created it: having conquered the land, calling it 'Algeria', and erecting a corresponding administrative and institutional state structure, the French could only be compelled to relinquish colonial control over the territory if a sufficiently powerful nationalist sentiment be generated – according to this argument. Algerian nationalism, as the inversion of French imperialism, came thus to be regarded as an ideological imperative for the attainment of independence; and independence was the pre-requisite for living according to Islamic values – such would be the justification for the combination of religion with nationalism effected by the reformist *'ulamā'*.

Furthermore, it is acknowledged by all serious analysts that the particular form of 'religious nationalism' propagated by the *'ulamā'* was in fact the bedrock of the revolution, giving to the natural religious motivation of the Algerian masses a political force that proved irresistible.[20] It is also clear that this religious impulse was 'hijacked' and exploited by the leftists during and after the war of independence.[21] It can also be maintained that the ensuing processes by which Algerian society was politicized and secularized had more to do with the dynamics within the new secular elites[22] than with the actions of the representatives of religion, who were soon marginalized. But to argue from these premises that today's Muslim extremists are simply the product of the political chaos and ideological fragmentation that characterized independent Algeria would not be warranted; for such a view overlooks the way in which religion itself had become so impoverished as to be rendered susceptible to the ideological pretensions of politically motivated groups. The corrosive influence of overt secularism ensured that religion would become marginalized, but this leaves open the question as to what it was that was being marginalized; for it was already an Islam that had been largely divested of its spiritual meaning that was placed on the sidelines by large sections of urban, educated society. This impoverishment of the meaning of religion on the socio-political plane cannot be dissociated from the prior diminution of the spirituality of the faith on the properly religious plane; and this, in turn, cannot be separated from the anti-Sufism campaign launched in the inter-war period by the reformist ʿulamāʾ in the name of 'purifying' Islam of all 'blameworthy innovations' (bidʿa).

It can be safely asserted that one of the consequences of this campaign is that today, for many if not most educated Algerians, Sufism is virtually synonymous with 'maraboutism' – saint-worshipping idolatry, superstitious donning of amulets, snake-charming, etc.; that is, Sufism not as it is in its essence or ideals, but such as it had become corrupted by small groups of pseudo-Sufis. A view of history now prevails in which the Sufis were the main agents of the 'decadence' from which Algerian society is yet to emerge.[23] According to the now common misconception, Sufis were superstitious marabouts who not only exploited the ignorant masses but also collaborated with the French. From this point of view, the Emir resisted the French despite his Sufism and not because of it; the fact that he was an eminent Sufi master is regarded as incidental to his greatness as a political leader. It is conveniently forgotten that, after the Emir, the stiffest military resistance to the French was mounted by the *Rahmānīyya* order in the Mokrani rebellion of the 1870s.[24] It is also forgotten that the French were so nervous about the political potential of Sufism that they formulated a deliberate policy, as noted by Omar Benaissa in Chapter 2, to pit the exoteric authorities against the Sufis. Finally, it is overlooked that, as Rashid Messaoudi pointed out in Chapter 1, it was the *zāwiyas* of the Sufis rather than the *madrasas* of the ʿulamāʾ that kept the spirit of Islam alive through the colonial period.[25]

While the piety of a great Sufi like the Shaykh al-ʿAlawī might be respected, his otherworldliness would be regarded as having been detrimental to the political imperative of liberation from French rule. It would be argued that the approach of Ben Bādīs, however much it might have unintentionally compromised the totality of the Islamic worldview, was nonetheless necessary for the time and the situation. On the other hand, the approach of the Sufis of the inter-war period was strictly speaking apolitical, and hence could not be proposed as an alternative 'strategy' of liberation.

One could reply to this argument as follows: noone would pretend that the activities of the Shaykh al-ʿAlawī and his like could have formed the basis for a political campaign aimed at achieving formal independence from the French; but this completely misses the point: even if the Shaykh was not concerned with beating the French politically, the French could not beat him psychologically, culturally, and spiritually. The underlying aim of French colonialism was to forge the Algerian personality in the image of French 'civilization';[26] and if one takes full account of the fact that the real danger of colonialism was cultural and psychological rather than merely political, being a mode of spiritual oppression more than a just a form of material exploitation – then this spiritual indomitability on the part of the Sufis assumes the dimensions of a signal victory. Indeed, the fidelity of the Sufis to the integral tradition of Islam might be said to constitute the most successful form of effective resistance to the secular designs of the French; for colonialism could make no psychological, moral, or cultural inroads into a mentality that remained inextricably rooted in the spiritual tradition of Islam. While others may have been more active in opposing the French politically, they nonetheless succumbed to the ways of thinking, acting, and even being that were proper to their secular overlords, of whom they thus became mirror-images: opponents in political form, allies in subconscious orientation.

Furthermore, given the fact that the rulers of 'independent' Algeria were far more successful than the French in establishing a secular, western-oriented culture within Algerian society, one wonders whether the attainment of political independence can in fact be said to constitute any 'victory' at all. It seems, rather, to have been a pyrrhic victory: power may have been won, but only for the sake of using it in order the better to attain the goals of one's erstwhile oppressors.

The 'strategy' of the Shaykh al-ʿAlawī might in fact be seen as the application, on the socio-cultural plane, of the following esoteric principle, enunciated by one of the great spiritual forefathers of the

Shaykh al-ʿAlawī, Mulay ʿAlī al-Jamal: 'The true way to hurt the enemy is to be occupied with the love of the Friend; on the other hand, if you engage in war with the enemy, he will have obtained what he wanted from you, and at the same time you will have lost the opportunity of loving the Friend.'[27] Lest this principle be regarded as a prescription for unconditional quietism, one should remember that the great *mujāhid* himself, the Emir ʿAbd al-Qādir, would have had no difficulty in assenting to this principle: for even while formally 'engaging' with the enemy on the battle-field, he was never for a moment distracted from his remembrance or his love of the 'Friend'. It was without bitterness and rage that he fought; and this explains the absence of bitterness in his soul towards the French when he was defeated by them, submitting to the manifest will of God with the same contemplative resignation with which he went into battle against them in the first place.[28] The contrast provided by the two 'strategies' of these great saints is more apparent than real: faced with different challenges, each adopted the tactics and the 'weapons' that appeared appropriate in the light of the circumstances. But the essential goal remained the same for both: safeguarding what remained of the integral Islamic tradition.

There is no doubt that the Shaykh al-ʿAlawī supported the general efforts of the reformists aiming at the restitution of Islamic institutions and culture; he indeed saw himself very much in the tradition of *tajdīd*, that is, renewal in a spiritual sense, raising the level of Islamic awareness and orientation. But instead of supporting the activities of the reformists, he was forced to defend Sufism against the blanket accusations that were levelled against it by them. He was the first to denounce the false mystics, the superstitions, and the heresies that gave Sufism a bad name; but he could not surrender the integral Sufi tradition to the reformist tendencies. For he saw clearly that these tendencies issued from an anti-spiritual perspective, one which could only have disastrous consequences for the tradition as a whole. For while the overt attacks on religion from without are clearly discernible as such, an attack on the spiritual tradition from within, in the name of reform, was a far more dangerous and insidious threat to the integrity of Islam. He asserted continually, according to his biographer, that 'of all the dangers which beset Islam, by far the greatest come from certain Moslems, and he makes it no secret that he is referring to those exoteric authorities of the group known as as-Salafiyyah who claimed to be 'reformers', a word which often aroused his anger and sarcasm, prompting him to quote from the Qoran: *And when it is said to them: "Cause not corruption in the land"*, *they say: "We are nothing if not reformers." Nay, unknown to themselves* *they are workers of corruption.'*[29]

It has been noted in Chapter 2 of this book that the Shaykh's spiritual radiance extended not just to a few disciples but, through his *muqaddams*, to hundreds of thousands of Muslims whose basic piety was deepened in a manner that cannot be quantified. It is important to stress the way in which this integral Sufism traditionally dovetailed with formal Islam, acting as a spiritual leaven for society as a whole, ensuring that observance of the Law is deepened by the assimilation of its inner Spirit. This synthesis between Shariʿite legality and Sufi spirituality in fact characterized the tradition of Maghrebi Islam for several centuries, and it was this synthesis that constituted the key obstacle in the path of 'progress', such as it was conceived by the Salafis.[30] They failed to appreciate the positive – indeed indispensable – social function that was performed by the type of Sufism associated with the likes of the Emir and the Shaykh al-ʿAlawī: at once intellectually penetrating, spiritually profound, and legally circumspect. For this form of Sufism not only satisfied the thirst for mystical experience and theosophical speculation among the spiritual 'travellers', but also served the concrete spiritual needs of ordinary people, and thus contributed to a social equilibrium that was suffused with a spiritual quality. In regard to the ʿAlawīyya in the 1930s, this social function can be seen to have operated at three distinct levels: at the level of the masses who were prone to lapse into spiritual lethargy, a tendency exacerbated by the fact of living under non-Muslim rule; at the level of the middle classes, traders, officers, civil servants, who were liable to be attracted by the material success and worldly efficiency of the colonizers; and at the level of the educated elite, who were then seeking answers to their deeper questions in the imported philosophies and ideologies of the West.

Rather than appreciate the positive role of Sufism, while simultaneously criticizing its decadent forms, the reformists saw nothing but the latter aspects: under the invisible sway of a modernist complex, Sufism as such became equated with backwardness, and had to be eliminated in the name of 'progress'. For the reformists attacked not just the abuses associated with maraboutism, but also practically everything connected with Sufism – the visiting of tombs of saints, the performing of mystical invocations, speculating on metaphysics: that is, the very things which the modern West had abandoned long ago. Although claiming to be going back to the forefathers,[31] the reformists were in fact more modernist, and even secularist, than they realized. For it must be remembered that secularism is not the direct antithesis of religion, as is atheism; rather it is a force which first marginalizes religion, and then enters into religion itself, which it ends up by falsifying. Religion subjected to secularism becomes, on the one hand, trivial, and on the other hand, horizontal. That is, secularized religion belittles, in existential terms, the manifestations of the sacred and, in doctrinal terms, all openings towards the transcendent.[32]

There is an important, if rather hidden, relationship between the relatively high number of Europeans who converted – and continue to convert – to Islam through Sufism, and the attack on Sufism by the Muslim reformers: it was the very element that was most evidently lacking in European society – the sacred – that proved most compelling to spiritually sensitive Europeans; and, conversely, it was the ramifications of this same element that most embarassed the reformers, for whom Islam had become not so much an outward form containing a spiritual essence as a form as such, an ideology, a system of actions and symbols, one that had to be defended against colonialism, on the one hand, and mystical 'obscurantism', on the other: that very obscurantism which the successful civilization of the West had purged from their religion long ago.

In fighting against the French, the Algerian reformist *'ulamā'* and the disenfranchized educated classes unconsciously absorbed from the French many implicit, underlying assumptions of what was modern and what was backward; consequently, they opposed those elements of their own culture that smacked of 'superstition' – defined implicitly in relation to what was 'progressive'. It was now 'superstitious' to kiss the hand of a spiritual master; to be detached from the world was 'irresponsible'; devotion to a spiritual discipline – the *jihād al-akbar* or greater Holy War – was 'selfish'; giving priority to contemplation over action was 'decadent'; engaging in invocation of the names of God – the central method of Sufism – was 'vain', while entering the forty-day spiritual retreat was sheer 'escapism' ... This was secularism through the back door, a subtle worldliness allied to religious formalism, the consequences of which became manifest in a palpable diminution of spirituality throughout society, but especially among the urban educated classes. Again, the objection will be made that this has more to do with the growth of secular norms, independent of religion, than with the consequences of the anti-Sufi campaign of the Salafis. But we would respond as follows: the rise in secularism is one thing, and the phenomenon of persons claiming to be religious while lacking any notion of authentic spirituality is another; the latter paradox cannot be dissociated from the deliberate downgrading, in the name of reformed religion, of the traditional forms taken by spirituality in Islam. One can gauge the extent of this diminution of spirituality by considering what might be the response of many formally 'religious' and politically active people today, to the following description of the Emir, given out as the conclusion to a pamphlet defining army regulations in 1839:

> Il Hadj Abdel Kader cares not for this world, and withdraws from it as much as his avocations will permit ... He rises in the middle of the night to recommend his own soul and the souls of his followers to God. His chief pleasure is in praying to God with fasting, that his sins may be forgiven ... When he administers justice, he hears complaints with the greatest patience ... when he preaches, his words bring tears to all eyes, and melt the hardest hearts. All who hear him become good Mussulmans.[33]

One should add here that the Emir not only remained faithful to the pure tradition of Sufism in intrinsic spiritual terms, but was also possessed of a keen intellectual discernment with regard to the false values of western civilization. In a remarkable document entitled *Letter to the French*, written after he was granted his freedom by Napoleon III, he showed that he was not at all impressed by the scientific and technological achievements of the French; they arose out of a spirit of practical application, he wrote, which could lead to 'damnable activities', whilst Islam, despite its decadence and material weakness, remained faithful to a spirit of metaphysical inquiry that opened onto knowledge of God. He thus urged the French, for their own good, to make an effort to understand Islam and its living spiritual tradition.34

Again, the contrast with the reformists of a century later is striking. For them, the 'progress' of Islam meant, in essence, the absorption of the material advances of western civilization within a form of religion that was liberated from the 'shackles' of a tradition deemed spiritually moribund. 'The Muslim is one who assumes progress', was the title of a poem of one of the favourite poets of the reformists, Muhammad Hadi Snusi, whose works adorned the pages of the reformist journal, *al-Shihāb*; and if one were to ask what was the meaning of this 'progress', the answer would be as follows: 'It is a fact that every time that the Algerian reformists treat of modernism (*tajdīd*) or of progress (*taqaddum*), they refer almost exclusively to material civilization.'35

If the gauge of 'progress' be material advancement, the inescapable corollary is that Muslim civilization be judged 'backward'; and everything within the civilization that resists the necessary drive to modernism must also be by definition 'regressive'. From the Emir's point of view, on the other hand, only that was 'backward' which turned its back on spiritual values, however much it may be advanced materially. In this connection, it is also useful to note the Emir's appreciation of the spiritual tradition of the West; after visiting the Church of Madeleine in Paris, he said: 'When I first began my struggle with the French, I thought they were a people without religion. I found out my mistake ... such churches as these would soon convince me of my error.'[36]

Whereas the Emir was dismissive of the material advantages of the West and respectful towards its spiritual tradition, today's Islamists are contemptuous of the tradition of the West while emulating its material success. There is here a stark contrast between an inferiority complex that derives from implicitly material standards, and an unshakeable certitude, derived from explicitly spiritual values. It might be said that today's Muslims suffer from this inferiority complex in the measure that their criterion of value is determined by material, 'horizontal' norms; while only those in the spiritual tradition, those who benefit concretely from the *baraka*, or grace, of that tradition, are able to share with the Emir the knowledge both of the intrinsic and immutable value of the Islamic civilization, and of the ways in which this civilization, despite its accidental decadence, is superior to modern civilization, despite its accidental advantages.

It might be objected that Sufism does not have a monopoly on Islamic spirituality; and that therefore the anti-Sufi campaign of the Salafis did not preclude the possibility of benefiting from the spiritual dimension of the faith. To this one would reply that Sufism is nothing but the crystallization of the spirituality of the Islamic tradition; to reject it is to reject that body of accumulated wisdom and experience that has been nourished principally on the most profound values of Islam, values that are in principle independent of Sufism *qua* historical phenomenon, but which Sufism helps to actualize and vivify for each succeeding generation. To reject this traditional wisdom means that one approaches the primary sources of religion not with the eyes of one who has cast off the blinkers of the past, but as one who will be looking through the distorting prism of contemporary norms; and this, in turn, translates into precisely the kind of inadvertent assimilation of modernism by those who claim to be 'reforming' religion.

***

Even if it be conceded that the reformists did impoverish Islam, it might still be argued that between their reduced form of religion and the outrages of today's Muslim extremists there is a great gulf; that the Salafis strictly upheld – and continue to uphold – the moral and legal principles of the faith even if their fidelity to its spirituality be questionable. The extremists will thus be held to have committed their immoral and illegal acts despite the influence of the Salafis and not because of it.

There are two responses that can be given to this argument. Firstly, many of the proponents and perpetrators of extremist violence belong to the group known as the 'Afghans', veterans from the anti-Soviet *jihād* of the 1980s; they are referred to, and indeed see themselves as 'Salafis', that is, continuing the original Salafi line of orientation, albeit to a degree that would be regarded as excessive by other Salafis.

Secondly, and more fundamentally, the influence of the Salafis was visible in the form of Islam adopted by the FLN at independence in 1962. Although, as has been noted above, the Islamic element in the war of independence was hijacked and then marginalized by the socialist elites that took control of the new state, there was nevertheless an assimilation of this reduced (anti-Sufi) version of Islam to the ruling socialist ideology. The political culture fostered by the Algerian state over two decades was one in which Islam was simultaneously exploited ideologically, excluded existentially, culturally, and intellectually, and further impoverished spiritually. It was in this environment that the first generation of independent Algerians was brought up. The seeds of ideologized Islam were sown in the minds of young people: fed on a diet of an Islam devoid of spiritual substance, on the one hand, and various shades of socialism replete with revolutionary overtones, on the other, the alienating effects of modernization and rapid urbanization were further exacerbated. If the specific ideological distortions of Islam can be attributed directly to the post-independence socialist and secular elites, the absence of a meaningful, valorized, and effective spiritual influence within urban culture – such as might have provided a countervailing force to the distortions of socio-political life – cannot be dissociated from the legacy of reformism.

As Lamchichi says, the independent Algerian state conducted a curious 'double discourse': on the one hand it was dominated by concepts such as 'laïcité', socialism, and 'Third World-ism', and on the other, by a truncated Islam, dismissive of Sufism and popular religion generally. 'In contrast to the religious policy of Morocco ... which does not a priori condemn all forms of popular religion (brotherhoods, cult of saints ...) the Algerian state has constantly attempted to impose a monist version ... of Islam, that is to say, that version considered as the sole orthodoxy on the religious plane.'37

Some fourteen years after the attainment of independence, the National Charter of 1976, 'popularly' acclaimed, tried to synthesise the two poles of this double discourse. The premise of the new synthesis was the following diagnosis: 'The decline of the Muslim world is not explained by purely moral causes ... In fact, in order to regenerate itself, the Muslim world has only one way out: to go beyond reformism and commit itself to the path of social revolution.'38

Reformism' – albeit an emasculated version thereof – was thus the platform from which must be launched an Islam that cohered with the demands of 'social revolution': just as the reformists had rejected those aspects of the tradition that did not conform to their modernizing designs, so the framers of Boumedienne's 'National Charter' felt the need to do to reformism what reformism had done to traditional Islam, to 'reform reformism', as it were, or rather, to revolutionize it. This task was not too difficult for, according to the Charter: 'Revolution indeed enters well in the historical perspective of Islam ... Muslim peoples will increasingly come to realize that it is in reinforcing their struggle against imperialism and engaging upon the path of socialism that they will best respond to the imperatives of their faith.'39 State-manipulated Islam – in various shades and flavours – served but to accelerate the exploitation of Islamic terms and symbols by increasingly diverse political groups, whose ideological innovations can be seen as extended images of the form of Islam sanctioned by the state, and whose fervour could thus be easily redirected away from the bogey of foreign imperialism to the corrupt elites governing their own state, as has happened in our times.

By the late 1970s, then, practically all that was left of the legacy of the reformists was the continuing disparagement of Sufism within the officially sanctioned parody of Islam. A representative of this 'official Islam' was Shaykh Hamami, President of the *Conseil Supérieur islamique*; he made plain this aversion to Sufism at the fourth congress of the FLN, convoked to appoint a successor to Boumedienne: 'Islam flows within us, and we flow in it. One cannot reduce it to liturgical rites, false appearances, it is not a religion of dervishes and charlatans, of ecstasy and dementia ... It is the religion of liberty ... and of democracy; no power [*hukm*] without consultation [*shūrā*].'[40]

The legacy of reformism is evident here in the rejection of Sufism by the derogatory use of the word 'dervishes' and in the mocking of their spiritual depth by referring to 'dementia' and 'ecstasy'; this clearly dovetails with the political reduction of Islam, now the religion not of salvation but of 'democracy': soteriology is now transformed into ideology. If Islam was viewed as a set of political rights to liberty and democracy, rather than a set of spiritual and moral duties to God, then, to be deprived of these rights by any state justifies, and indeed compels, the good Muslim to political action – extreme, if need be – against such an un-Islamic state.

***

It has been asserted in the first part of this essay that it was the politics of repression that explained the rise of Islamist violence; but it is also necessary to mention here that the socio-economic conditions that prevailed from the middle of the 1980s onwards helped actualize not only the latent 'revolutionary Islam' fostered by state ideology, but also the Islamist movement generally, that is, the moderate, democratic, gradualist form of Islam to which the vast majority of the Algerian Islamists adhere. While it was true that the political rights enshrined in official party ideology were in fact never granted the Algerian people, this was partly compensated by the populist form of socialism that at least guaranteed certain socio-economic rights; a rough and ready egalitarianism was the reward for submission to the one-party state. But once this populism was dropped from the party agenda, and a crude version of free market capitalism was adopted in its stead, there ensued a reduction of social security and cuts in basic food subsidies, on the one hand, and a massive rise in economic disparities, unemployment, and black market profiteering on the other.[41] The frustrations generated by this unbalanced economic development, coupled with the emergence of more fully democratic procedures in politics, fuelled the growth of Islamism as the principal expression of a collective desire for fundamental change.

One should repeat that the Islamist movement in Algeria was essentially peaceful and gradualist, with extremist factions reined in by the mainstream until 1992; however much one may take issue with the lack of spiritual depth of the FIS, whose programme is in so many ways a political prolongation of that of the reformists whom they claim as their precursors and inspirers, their non-violent approach to politics must be acknowledged: the violence of the GIA must not be allowed to discredit the Islamist movement as a whole, at least insofar as purely political strategy is concerned. This violence, although it emerged from the bosom of the peaceful version of Islam proposed by the FIS, nonetheless shares with the FIS the underlying politicized conception of religion which was the fruit both of direct Salafi reductionist influence, and of the secular state's exploitation of a distorted version of 'reformed' Islam.

***

CONCLUSION

At the present moment, those involved in the Algerian Islamist movement are naturally pre-occupied more with the imperatives of survival than with the subtleties of Islam. But, insofar as Islam really does enter into their thinking, they cannot absolve themselves of the duty to condemn in the strongest possible terms the terrorist actions committed in the name of Islam. In the absence of such condemnation, their movement becomes distinguishable only in name from any other insurrection aimed purely at winning political power.

But anti-terrorism is only one component of an authentic approach to the restoration of Islamic values; what is evidently lacking in the Islamist movement in Algeria and elsewhere in the Muslim world is a spiritual dimension. On the one hand this absence of spiritual depth is a cause of the dismissal of Sufism by politically active Islamists, and on the other hand, it is itself a consequence of the rejection of Sufism by significant sections of two generations of Algerians. It is not realized that Sufism, far from being a relic of the past, is a still-living element of Islam, capable of exercising its traditional role: that of infusing into society at large those spiritual values that constitute the very *raison d'être* of Islam, and without which the concepts and practices of the faith can so easily become encrusted in formalism, reduced to superficiality, shrouded in hypocrisy, or subverted by fanaticism.

Perhaps the single greatest prejudice against Sufism, drummed in by decades of reformist influence and state propaganda, is that Sufism is irrelevant to today's world, incapable of providing solutions to the complex problems of modern life. In addition to the principial points made above, one might cite by way of response, the example of the *Būshishīyya ṭarīqa* (a branch of the *Qādirīyya*) in neighbouring Morocco. Professor Mohammed Tozy analysed the teaching methods of the order, which boasts a membership of over one hundred thousand. He noted an impressive combination of classical texts and modern subjects in the curriculum, and, after closely observing over a period of four years the progress of a dozen students aged between twenty and twenty-five years, he remarked:

> What distinguished them from other students was a great serenity and the absence of anxiety with regard to the future. I was also very surprised by the quality of their formation, at once Sufi and academic, which produced for them great confidence and a capacity to function on several planes (training, organisation, exegesis, psalmody of the Qur'an, recitation of mystical poems, political and even scientific analyses).[42]

The example of the *Būshishīyya* is, according to Tozy, replicated on an increasingly large-scale throughout Morocco; and this to such an extent that he feels justified in referring to the phenomenon as 'neo-turuqism': an autonomous development and institutionalization of popular *and* scholarly, even 'scientific', Sufism that both satisfies perennial spiritual needs and offers solutions to contemporary problems. But more fundamentally, the persistence of the stabilizing influence of traditional Sufism has been a major reason why Moroccan society has been spared the ravages experienced by Algeria, and why Moroccan Islamist trends have been peaceful hitherto.

Algeria has also experienced a marked rise in the activities and significance of the Sufi brotherhoods, as noted by Sossie Andezian in Chapter V. Although largely overlooked by outside commentators because of its lack of sensationalism, this resurgence of Sufism should not be regarded simply as an appendage to the rise of political Islam, but as an invaluable resource in the attempt to restore a properly spiritual sense of values, something from which Muslims of all persuasions can benefit.

It has been noted that the Algerian state has recently begun to support the activities of the brotherhoods, this being part of its strategy to disentangle Islamic discourse from the FIS, shifting it onto a more 'safe' territory, that of state Islam on the one hand and apolitical Sufism on the other. Now it would be the height of spiritual hypocrisy for Islamists to oppose the revival of Sufism simply on the political calculation that 'the enemy's friend is our enemy'. Mohamed Gharib calls, at the end of his essay in this volume, for a 'historic compromise' between all parties to the conflict; we would amplify this call, adding that there must be compromise not just between the state and the Islamists, but also between different groups within that large segment of the populace that genuinely seeks a restoration of authentic Islamic values, and thus a compromise between Islamists and Sufis.[43]

One is not necessarily arguing here that Islamists ought to learn from Sufis how to conduct their political activities; only that without the presence of the spiritual values on which Sufism is predicated, political activities in the name of Islam are inevitably going to be more political than Islamic, with the ever-present danger of a slide into unprincipled violence. Those who would be 'reformers' of Islam should realize that reform of religion always presupposes reform of the individual, and such reform is the domain, *par excellence*, of Sufism, which, aiming at inculcating virtue and piety in the soul, cannot but have beneficial consequences for society as a whole, while the converse does not hold: a political campaign aimed at changing society does not necessarily result in the spread of virtue and piety.

God will not change the condition of a people until they change the condition of their own souls. (The Qur'ān, XIII: 11.)ᴄᴡ

NOTES

1. Quoted in Charles Henry Churchill, *The Life of Abdel Kader*, London: Chapman and Hall, 1867, p. 323. These words were written by the Emir in a letter regarding his defence of the Christians fleeing a pogrom in Damascus in 1860, about which more will be said below. Regarding the quotation made by the Emir, it appears to be from the *sūra Yūsuf*, verse 18; we have taken the liberty therefore of amending Churchill's rather loose translation of *ṣabrun jamīlun, wa'Llāhu'l-musta'ān*, which he rendered as 'patience is lovable; in God let us trust.'

2. By 'political culture' is intended that cluster of associated values and assumptions that define the parameters, the place, and the basic situation in which political action occurs. This is a modified version of the well known definition of political culture given by Sidney Verba, 'Comparative Political Culture', p. 513, in L.W. Pye and S. Verba, *Political Culture and Political Development*, Princeton University Press, 1965.

3. This designation is used generically to describe all those whose overriding goal is the political restoration of an Islamic order – however this be defined, and whatever be the strategy chosen to implement this objective. It thus encompasses both moderates and extremists. For a useful discussion and definition of the term, see

François Burgat, *L'islamisme au Mahgreb*, Paris: Karthala, 1988, pp. 52-55.

4. Our comments are based on the penetrating analyses of François Burgat; in addition to the work cited above, see his *L'islamisme en face*, Paris: Éditions La Découverte, 1995.

5. See for details, *Livre blanc sur la répression en Algérie*, by Le ComitÈ Algérien des Militants Libres de la Dignité Humaine et des Droits de l'Homme, Geneva: Éditions Hoggar, 1996.

6. Prior to this repression, as Burgat argues, the level of Islamist violence in Algeria was minimal. See *L'islamisme en face*, op.cit., p. 159. The only significant extremist group in the 1980s was the *Mouvement Islamic Armé*, led by Mustapha Bouyali, who was killed by security forces in 1987. (See Hugh Roberts, 'Algeria between Eradicators and Conciliators', *Middle East Research and Information Project*, July-August, 1994, p. 24.) The existence of this group at a time when state repression was not so intense will probably be dismissed by today's Islamists as an aberration; but from our point of view, it only serves to underline the need for a properly religious critique: for the resort to illegal and unjustified violence in the name of Islam did not emerge out of a vacuum, and still less out of a traditional Islamic ambience; rather, it must be seen as the product of a political environment within which religion was already but a political shadow of its true self.

7. Reports are circulating to the effect that the recently killed 'Emir' of the GIA was in fact a member of the state security forces; this is all too credible, given the unprincipled nature of the Algerian security forces. But whether or not this is true has little bearing on the critique at the level of Islamic principles; the fact that his ideas found a following among young Muslims is sufficient evidence of the malaise with which we are concerned.

8. See for details, *L'Algérie en murmure. Un Cahier sur la torture*, Moussa Ait-Embarek, Geneva: Editions Hoggar, 1996.

9. *L'islamisme en face*, op.cit., pp. 164-165; this paragraph was translated by Rashid Messaoudi.

10. Even though these denunciations have not been widely

reported in the western media.

11. Roberts, 'Algeria between Eradicators and Conciliators', op.cit., p. 26.

12. Quoted in Mohamed Chérif Sahli, *Abdelkader - Le Chevalier de la Foi*, Algiers: Entreprise algérienne de presse, 1967, pp. 131-132. It is instructive to note that, among the hundreds of French admirers who payed their respects to the Emir in France – after he had been defeated by the French and was in France, prior to leaving for the East – the visitors by whom he was deeply touched were French officers who came to thank him for the kind treatment they received at his hands when they were his prisoners in Algeria. See Churchill, op.cit., p. 295.

13. Sahli, op.cit., p. 132.

14. Churchill, op.cit., p. 314.

15. Ibid., p. 318.

16. It is interesting to note that another great Sufi master, Imam Shamil of Daghestan, who by this time had also been defeated after his heroic stand against the Russians, wrote a letter to the Emir, praising him for his noble action, and thanking God that there were still Muslims who behaved according to the high spiritual ideals of the faith. In the context of the present discussion, it is worth quoting the following passage from the Imam's letter:

I was astonished at the blindness of the functionaries who have plunged into such excesses, forgetful of the words of the Prophet, peace be upon him, 'Whoever shall be unjust towards a tributary (a Christian), who shall do him a wrong, who shall lay on him any charge beyond his means, and finally, who shall deprive him of anything without his own consent, it is I who will be his accuser in the day of judgment.'

See Churchill, op.cit., p. 321-322.

17. Quoted on p. 123 of *L'Islam entre Tradition et Révolution*, Roger du Pasquier, Paris: Éditions Tougui, 1987.

18. From the journal *al-Muntaqid*, 1925. Quoted in George A. Taliadoros, *La Culture Politique Arabo-Islamique et la Naissance du Nationalisme Algérien (1830-1962)*, p.50. Algiers: Entreprise Nationale du Livre, 1985. (This writer's translation.)

19. It might be said that individualism fills the vacuum created by the spread of secularism: where religion explicitly posits the submission of the individual to the Absolute, secularism implicitly absolutizes the individual, with all the social divisiveness that this entails.

20. See A. Humbaraci, *Algeria: A Revolution That Failed*, London: Pall Mall Press, 1966, pp. 26-68. René Delisle claims that the *ʿulamāʾ*, in shaping the thinking of thousands of young men, produced 'the essential armature of the nationalist movement'; according to Jean-Claude Vatin, independent Algeria was the achievement of the *ʿulamāʾ*, the armed struggle against the French being the culmination of their teachings over the previous thirty years. For these and other similar opinions, see Taliadoros, op.cit., p. 53.

21. According to Mohamed Lebjaoui, a leader of the National Liberation Front (FLN), the leaders of the revolution were right to utilize this religious fervour for the struggle, and that they also knew how to eliminate 'religious fanaticism' so as to 'pose the Algerian problem on a strictly national, rather than a racial or narrowly religious plane.' *Verités sur la Révolution algérienne*, Paris: Gallimard, 1970; quoted in Ibid., p. 63. (This writer's translation.)

22. For a useful overview of the social processes to which successive generations of Algerian elites were subjected, and a clear explanation of the intra-elite conflicts that have bedevilled Algerian politics, see W. B. Quandt, *Revolution and Political Leadership: Algeria, 1954-68*, Cambridge, Mass., and London: MIT Press, 1972.

23. An extreme but not untypical assessment of Algerian history is given by Mahmoud Bennoune: Algeria, he writes, is under 'the weight of a thousand years of decadence', corrupted not only by ignorant politicians, but also 'lazy and brutalized ideologues ... and obscurantist religious zealots preaching obsolete ideologies designed to drag us back into dead ages'. It would not have been necessary to spell out for his readers that the zealots he has in mind are Sufis. From page 42 of his chapter 'Socio-historical Foundations of the Contemporary Algerian State', in Ali El-Kenz, (ed.) *Algeria: The Challenge of Modernity*, London: Codesria, 1991.

24. See Peter von Sivers, 'Insurrection and Accomodation: Indigenous leadership in Eastern Algeria, 1840-1900' in *International Journal of Middle Eastern Studies*, VI, 1975.

25. It should also be noted that Sufism played a significant role in deepening the commitment of the Berber tribes to Islam. According to Charles-Robert Ageron, Islam was 'rooted in the affections of the population by the Sufi brotherhoods or *ṭuruq*, the marabouts (*murābiṭūn*) or holy men and the *shurafā'*, descendants of the Prophet. It was these brotherhoods and lineages which ... progressively Islamized and gradually Arabized the lands of the Berbers.' *Modern Algeria*, (Tr. Michael Brett), London: Hurst, 1991, pp. 1-2. See also, for an account of the spread of Sufism more generally throughout the Berber domains of the Maghreb, Alfred Bel, *La Religion Musulmane en Berbérie*, Paris: Orientaliste Paul Geuthner, 1938, pp. 331-356.

26. It is important to note the dissenting French voices within France and Algeria to the crude version of assimilation that prevailed in public policy. The renowned historian and sociologist Alexis de Tocqueville argued, in a parliamentary report of 1847, that 'We should not at present push them [the natives] along the path of our own European civilization, but in the direction of their own.' He bitterly criticized the assimilationist French policy then in force in Algeria: 'We have cut down the number of charities, let schools fall into ruin, closed the colleges ... the recruitment of the men of religion and of the law has ceased. We have, in other words, made Muslim society far more miserable, disorganized, ignorant and barbarous than ever it was before it knew us.' Quoted in Ageron, op.cit., p. 21. Other proponents of 'association', as opposed to 'assimilation' were Napoleon III – reviled by the colons as the 'Emperor of the Arabs' – General Fleury, Colonel Lapasset, the convert Thomas-Ismail Urbain and, in the 1890s, Jules Ferry and Jules Cambon, Governor of Algeria 1891-1897. See idem. for details.

27. Quoted by the great dsciple of Mulay al-Jamal, the Shaikh al-ʿArabī al-Darqāwī, the founder of the Darqāwī branch of the Shādhilī order. *Letters of a Sufi Master* (Tr. T. Burckhardt), Bedfont, Middlesex: Perennial Books, 1969, p. 9. Albeit on a much lower level, Hourani

expresses something similar to this rule, when he writes: 'Polemics have their danger: in defending oneself, one may draw closer to one's adversary than one thinks.' Quoted in Julian Johansen, *Sufism and Islamic Reform: The Battle for the Islamic Tradition*, Oxford University Press, 1996, p. 15.

28. One cannot help recalling here the story told of the great hero of early Islam, ʿAlī ibn Abū Ṭālib, such as it has been recounted in the Islamic tradition. He was on the point of delivering the death-blow to an enemy on the ground, when his defeated foe spat at him; ʿAlī sheathed his sword calmly. Upon being asked by his opponent why he did not kill him, ʿAlī replied that had he done so at that moment he would have killed out of personal anger, and not for the sake of God. Herein lies a much needed lesson for today's would-be *mujāhidīn*. The true warrior of Islam fights fiercely, when he has to, but without his inward detachment and serenity being disturbed by any egotistic zeal.

29. M. Lings, *A Sufi Saint of the Twentieth Century, Shaikh Aḥmad al-ʿAlawī*, London: George Allen & Unwin, 1971, pp. 108-109. The Qur'ānic quotation is from II: 11-12.

30. 'The major target of the reformist attacks was really the medieval synthesis – both the unchanging, intellectually dessicated, official 'learned' class [i.e, the ʿulamāʾ], and the Sufi movement.' Leon Carl Brown, 'The Islamist Reform Movement in North Africa', in *Journal of Modern African Studies*, II,1, 1964, p. 58. Brown also notes that most of the ʿulamāʾ belonged to Sufi orders, as did most of the rulers (ibid., p.56). From around the 14th century onwards, any student pursuing a course of advanced religious studies would invariably find Sufism included in the curriculum (see Bel, 'La Religion Mussulmane', op.cit., p. 330.) This traditional synthesis contained a creative tension between the two poles of tradition: whereas the antinomian tendencies within Sufism can stray into heresy without the stabilizing influence of the Law, legalism can become unilateral, rigid, and fanatical unless vivified from within by the influence of Sufism.

31. *Al-salaf al-ṣāliḥ* means literally the 'pious forefathers' and refers

to the early generations of Islam; for a useful evaluation of the anti-Sufi attitude of one of the most important leaders of the Salafis, Rashīd Riḍā, see Albert Hourani's chapter 'Sufism and Modern Islam: Rashid Rida', in his *The Emergence of the Modern Middle East*, London: MacMillan, 1981. It is interesting to note that Riḍā's master, Muḥammad ʿAbduh, one of the leading lights of the Salafi movement, had a less critical stance as regards Sufism. He distinguished between authentic Sufis and their corrupt imitators, defining the former as 'those whose concern is the rectification (*iṣlāḥ*) of hearts, the purification of their innermost selves (*sarāʾir*) and the spiritual reception of the exalted and majestic Countenance of Truth, so that they are drawn to Him by divine attraction, [losing sight of] all others. Their essence (*dhāt*) is extinguished in His Essence, their characteristics in His. The sages (*ʿārifūn*) amongst them who reach the end of their journey attain to the highest degree of human perfection after the prophets.' Quoted in J. Johansen, *Sufism and Islamic Reform*, op.cit., p. 21. This nuanced approach notwithstanding, the influence of the school associated with ʿAbduh has been distinctly and almost indiscriminately anti-Sufi, particularly in modern times.

32. One has only to look at the Christian Church in our times to see how, far from determining the essential character of society, religion in the West apes the ever-changing intellectual fashions of secular society, to the point where bishops can deny the Virgin Birth of Christ, and priests can bless homosexual marriages. For a profound critique of secular western norms, in particular the idea of 'progress', see M. Lings, *Ancient Beliefs and Modern Superstitions*. Cambridge: Quinta Essentia, 1991.

33. Translated by Churchill, op.cit., pp. 137-138. See also Raphael Danziger, *Abd al-Qadir and the Algerians*, New York: Homes & Meier, 1977, p. 181.

34. Quoted in Du Pasquier, op.cit., p. 6.

35. Ali Merad, *Le Réformisme Musulman en Algérie, de 1925 á 1940*, Paris/The Hague: Mouton, 1967, p. 308. (Translation by this writer.)

36. From Churchill, op.cit., p. 295

37. Abderrahim Lamchichi, *L'Islamisme en Algérie*, Paris; Éditions

L'Harmattan, 1992, p. 63-64. (Translated by this writer.)

38. Quoted in Hugh Roberts, 'Radical Islamism and the Dilemma of Algerian Nationalism', *Third World Quarterly*, April, 1988, vol.10, no.2, p. 571.

39. Quoted in Du Pasquier, op.cit., pp. 105-6. (This writer's translation.)

40. Quoted on p. 63 of ibid.

41. See, for a useful overview of this transition, Ali El-Kenz, 'Algerian Society Today: A Phenomenological Essay on the National Consciousness', pp. 21-33, in *Algeria: The Challenge of Modernity*, op.cit.

42. Mohammed Tozy, 'Le prince, le clerc at l'état', p. 86, in *Intellectuels et militants de L'islam contemporain*, G. Kepel, Y. Richard (eds.), Paris: Éditions du Seuil, 1990. (This writer's translation.)

43. A comparison between Algeria and Turkey in this respect is quite useful. The rise of political Islam in Turkey during the past two decades has been closely tied to the growing influence of the Naqshbandī order, an influence which has doubtless helped to moderate the movement, even if the relationship between the leaders of the respective trends – political and spiritual – has not always been harmonious; and even if the spiritual side of the partnership might be criticized for having become excessively worldly. See the essays by Hakan Yavuz and Hamid Algar, and the interview with Abdullah Gül in *Turkey: The Pendulum Swings Back*, Islamic World Report, Vol.1 No.3, 1996. It is of course also true that the fact that the military refrained from intervention, and allowed the Refah Party to form a coalition government several months after its victory at the general election of December 1995, was an important factor in the continuing moderation of the Islamists in Turkey. The contrast between Algeria and Turkey is full of political significance: on the one hand the Islamist movement is given political expression within the prevailing political system, and remains moderate, rational and gradualist; on the other hand it is savagely repressed and excluded from the political system, with the result that the moderates in the movement are eclipsed by the extremists who respond to the regime's violence in kind.

NOTE ON CONTRIBUTORS

SOSSIE ANDEZIAN is Research Supervisor at the *Centre National de la Recherche Scientifique* in France. She is also attached to a Research Unit in Marseilles, *Sociologie, Histoire, Anthropologie des Dynamiques Culturelles* (SHADYC). She has worked for many years in the field of Sufism and popular Islam in western Algeria.

OMAR BENAISSA, a Berber from Algeria, has carried out extensive research on Sufism; he is currently completing a doctoral thesis on the influence of the School of Ibn Arabi in Persia, under the direction of Charles-Henri de Fouchécour, at the Sorbonne Nouvelle University in Paris.

MOHAMED GHARIB, of Algerian origin, is a freelance writer on Algerian and Islamic affairs.

GEORGE JOFFÉ specializes in North African Affairs and is the Honorary Secretary of the Society of Moroccan Studies. He is also attached to the Geopolitics and International Boundaries Research Centre at the School of Oriental and African Studies in London University.

MICHÈLE MESSAOUDI edits and translates books on Islam, lectures on various aspects of the Islamic tradition, has been head-teacher of an Islamic school, and has written several children's books.

RASHID MESSAOUDI, from Algeria, is a writer on political affairs, an editor and professional translator.

BRAHIM S. NALI, a Berber from Algeria, is a freelance writer and editor.

REZA SHAH-KAZEMI is a freelance writer and editor and specializes in comparative religion.